Team Writing

A Guide to Working in Groups

Team Writing

A Guide to Working in Groups

Joanna Wolfe
University of Louisville

Bedford / St. Martin's
Boston ◆ *New York*

For Bedford/St. Martin's

Executive Editor: Leasa Burton
Developmental Editor: Sarah Guariglia
Production Editor: Annette Pagliaro Sweeney
Production Supervisor: Ashley Chalmers
Marketing Manager: Molly Parke
Copyeditor: Linda McLatchie
Project Management, Text Design, and Composition: Books By Design, Inc.
Senior Art Director: Anna Palchik
Cover Design: Richard DiTomassi
Printing and Binding: RR Donnelley & Sons Company

President: Joan E. Feinberg
Editorial Director: Denise B. Wydra
Director of Marketing: Karen R. Soeltz
Director of Editing, Design, and Production: Marcia Cohen
Assistant Director of Editing, Design, and Production: Elise S. Kaiser
Managing Editor: Elizabeth M. Schaaf

Library of Congress Control Number: 2009924655

Manufactured in the United States of America.

9   8   7
p o n

For information, write: Bedford/St. Martin's, 75 Arlington Street, Boston, MA 02116   (617-399-4000)

ISBN-10: 0-312-56582-8
ISBN-13: 978-0-312-56582-4

Acknowledgment
Microsoft® product screen shots reprinted with permission from Microsoft.

Preface

Team Writing is a brief guide about how to collaborate to produce a major written document. This book grew out of a research project, funded by the National Science Foundation, to discover factors that limited women's participation on technical teams. The ultimate goal of this project was to develop and test pedagogical strategies that would improve women's experiences on technical teams. However, as I and my research assistants observed 17 teams in technical writing and engineering classes, we were dumbfounded by the sheer number and scope of the problems we observed at all levels of the team process. Certainly we saw many gender-related problems, but far more compelling were the major breakdowns in collaboration—for example, students missing meetings and then complaining to instructors that their teammates were not keeping them informed; a student so defensive about his writing that he resisted fixing even basic grammatical errors; teams that to us looked as though they were proceeding logically and productively, only to discover later that some of the team members were angry and resentful because they didn't feel empowered to suggest changes to work that others produced; teams that started out with great and ambitious ideas but ended up throwing the project together sloppily at the last minute because nobody had written these agreements down. In all, nearly half the teams we observed experienced major breakdowns such as these.

Perhaps even more disturbing was the fact that the instructors responsible for these teams were rarely aware of the problems students were facing. Students almost never notified instructors of these problems or consulted them for advice—no matter how bad their team's problems might be—and instructors had no independent information that could help them anticipate and head off trouble. It became clear that students needed guidance and structure, which instructors were unaware they had to explicitly provide.

To address these issues, *Team Writing* focuses on the role of written communication in teamwork. It teaches students how to use written documentation to manage a team by producing task schedules, minutes, charters, and other materials and also provides models for handling the writing, research, and revision that large collaborative documents require. This focus on writing and teamwork is unique: whereas most textbooks that address team skills focus almost exclusively on verbal, face-to-face communication (which is just one, and not even the largest, aspect of a collaborative project), *Team Writing* draws on published research, observations and interviews with student teams, and my own experience in the classroom to show how written communication is not merely an afterthought but is the substance of most team activities.

A unique feature of this textbook is the inclusion of five short videos based on actual team interactions. These short vignettes allow students to see firsthand some of the problems teams can face. In the end-of-chapter exercises, students are asked to analyze the teams' behavior, providing hands-on opportunities to put some of the book's principles into action. These short videos reenact dialogue and behaviors observed in real student teams. Although in some cases the original interactions were modified slightly to remove distractions or clarify details, the dialogue remains faithful to the look and feel of the original groups' exact words and actions. These videos are further supplemented by comments that team members made at the end of the project or by observations from professional managers who viewed the videos.

Throughout the book, you will find examples of students' own words as they encounter and then solve problems on their teams. The book offers specific advice for avoiding these problems, as well as many examples of e-mails and documents that students can use as models for handling common situations. The troubleshooting guide inside the back cover lists some of the problems that this book teaches students to overcome.

This book, which is intended as a supplement to other course texts, has eight short chapters. The entire textbook, including all exercises, could be completed within the span of a two-week unit. Alternatively, the text could be spaced out over the course of a major project to correspond with issues that teams will be tackling at each stage of the project. Students can view the accompanying videos and respond to the exercises as independent homework, or they can watch the videos with their peers in class as a way to spark discussion on issues such as how to organize a project, respond to revisions, deal with people with different communication styles, or handle teammates who will not listen. These videos, as well as copies of the worksheets and some of the sample documents mentioned in the text, can be downloaded at the text Web site at <bedfordstmartins.com/teamwriting>.

◆ Acknowledgments

Grateful acknowledgment is made for the support of the National Science Foundation, Grant No. HRD-0225186. However, the flaws are my own, and any opinions, findings, and conclusions or recommendations expressed in this material are my own and do not necessarily reflect the views of the National Science Foundation.

I am particularly grateful to my two research assistants, Kara Alexander and Elizabeth Powell, who helped me collect and analyze the massive amount of data involved in this project and have worked with me to pilot and troubleshoot the materials contained in this book. I have been privileged to work with them, and this book owes much to their insights and observations. I am also greatly indebted to the many students and instructors who allowed me into their classrooms and permitted me and my assistants to observe their interactions. Thanks are also due to Ruta Sevo, Randall Walker, and Keith Ware, who provided their professional insights into the team process and commented on the videos. I would also like to thank the student actors who participated in the videos, as well as Mike Peak, who provided his technical and artistic support and advice in creating the videos.

I also want to acknowledge my appreciation for the reviewers who commented specifically on this manuscript: Jennifer Courtney, Rowan University; Doug Eyman, George Mason University; Susan Grover, Brigham Young University–Idaho; Ann Jennings, University of Houston–Downtown; Michael Knievel, University of Wyoming; William Lenox, Johnson & Wales University; Karen Powers Liebhaber, Black River Technical College; Steve Lytle, University of Central Florida; Ron McNeel, New Mexico State University at Alamogordo; Becky Jo McShane, Weber State University; Derek Mueller, Syracuse University; Paul Pedroza, University of Illinois–Urbana-Champaign; Janine Solberg, University of Massachusetts Amherst; Gretchen Vik, San Diego State University; Audrey Wick, Blinn College; John Zuern, University of Hawaii at Manoa; and one anonymous reviewer.

I am also indebted to the staff at Bedford/St. Martin's for their expert and thoughtful advice in shaping this book. Leasa Burton helped launch this project and provided her advice and vision as executive editor. Sarah Guariglia steered this project, providing exceptional editorial advice, insights, and encouragement. Her work was first-rate, and I cannot thank her enough. Dan Schwartz provided expert advice and assistance with the videos. My thanks also go to Joan Feinberg, Denise Wydra, and Karen Henry for their direction and help in making this a pleasurable project. Thanks also to Annette Pagliaro Sweeney and Nancy Benjamin for guiding the manuscript through production, Linda McLatchie for careful copyediting, and Anna Palchik and Janis Owens for the design work.

About the Author

Joanna Wolfe (PhD, University of Texas at Austin) is Associate Professor of English at the University of Louisville, where she teaches undergraduate and graduate courses in writing, and in rhetoric and composition. She is the author of numerous scholarly articles on teamwork, gender studies, collaborative learning technology, and technical writing appearing in forums such as *Journal of Engineering Education, Journal of Business and Technical Communication,* and *Written Communication.* Her research on collaborative writing in technical communication classes won the 2006 National Council of Teachers of English (NCTE) award for best article reporting qualitative or quantitative research in technical and scientific communication.

Contents

Team Writing

A Guide to Working in Groups

PART 1

Before You Start

CHAPTER 1

Planning Your Collaboration

At the end of a semester-long project on advanced database techniques, Eduardo, a graduate student in computer science, reflected on his team's collaboration:

> **Interviewer:** *Did anybody give you any input on the sections of the report that you wrote?*
> **Eduardo:** *No. No, nobody gave their opinion on anybody's work.*
> **Interviewer:** *Did you expect them to?*
> **Eduardo:** *Well, at the beginning, yes . . . but then everybody submitted at the last minute, so it was rushed. Umm, also we didn't have a chance 'cause we didn't meet after we submitted the draft. At that point, we were in finals, and we weren't going to do anything else.*
> **Interviewer:** *How do you think your teammates would evaluate your contribution?*
> **Eduardo:** *Well, I would hope they would say I did the most, but I don't know. I don't think some of them read [the final report].*

Thomas, a biology student in a technical writing class, also feels that his collaborative project did not live up to his expectations:

> **Thomas:** *Personally, I thought we could have used class time better.*
> **Interviewer:** *How so?*
> **Thomas:** *Because I think we could have got more of it done outside of class. . . . It took us 50 minutes to revise about half a page because of word choice or how we wanted to say it. I think that we thought we were actually more ahead than what we were . . . and then the final deadline caught up to us. It snuck up on us.*

Susan, an undergraduate majoring in math, similarly expresses frustration with a collaborative project she worked on in her technical writing class:

Interviewer: *So how did you decide who was going to do what?*

Susan: *Well, originally we all decided that we were gonna get together and do the Web site, but Rene took the disc and drafted the site herself. And then the rest of the project was just kind of, we volunteered for stuff as it came up, I guess.*

Interviewer: *And how did you feel about that?*

Susan: *It kind of destroyed our group working together. . . . We were going to do it all together because none of us knew how to do a Web site, and then Rene just went and did it all . . . and then she had to come back and explain it to us.*

These three students—and all the other students discussed in this book—were members of actual student teams observed as they worked on team projects in technical writing and engineering classes. Like the majority of the teams observed, these student groups had problems working together toward a common end. In some cases, students weren't aware of what their teammates had done, other teams failed to budget their time effectively, and still other teams ended up with hurt feelings and resentment. This textbook is intended to teach you to replace such frustrating team situations with ones where you coordinate with your teammates to produce work that is better and much more innovative than what any one of you could have created on your own.

This book focuses on the role of writing in effective teamwork. First, you will learn to produce the types of internal team documents that are *absolutely essential* to a well-run project—documents such as task schedules, meeting minutes, and team agendas as well as e-mails and memos that help head off potential problems. Second, you will learn how to write and revise large documents as a group. This focus on large documents is important because so much collaboration in fields like engineering, business, computer science, medicine, and hard sciences (to name a few) involves major written documents such as design plans, proposals, reports, manuals, and Web sites. This book teaches you specific writing strategies for managing such large documents.

Before you continue reading, take a moment to review the three preceding scenarios and reflect on why these student teams experienced breakdowns. What could these teams have done differently to prevent the problems they experienced?

◆ Why Teamwork?

These three scenarios illustrate the various problems that student teams can encounter. Given the problems with collaboration, why do teachers assign team projects in the first place? Group projects are typically assigned in school for two reasons:

1. To prepare students for the workplace by providing opportunities to learn the social and organizational skills necessary for productive teamwork. Employers in many fields want to hire graduates who already have experience working collaboratively.

2. To improve the educational experience through collaboration with fellow students. Educational research suggests that people learn the most when working with peers toward a common goal. When students discuss problems with an instructor or someone else who is considered an expert, they tend to automatically defer to the expert's viewpoint. However, when students discuss problems with peers, they are freer to debate and think through the problem and all the issues involved.

Let's take each of these reasons separately. First, collaboration has become the norm in most workplaces. On large, complex projects, no one person has all of the expertise and experience (let alone time and energy) to complete the project by himself or herself. Even smaller projects tend to take advantage of teamwork. People working together can often produce better outcomes in less time than any one person could produce independently. Team members benefit from a diversity of approaches and perspectives that lead to innovative insights.

However, teams often fail to work together effectively—and that failure threatens the entire project. For instance, Tom DeMarco and Timothy Lister (1987), experienced software specialists, write:

> The success or failure of a project is seldom due to technical issues. . . .
> If the project goes down the tubes it will be non-technical, human interaction problems that do it in. The team will fail to bind, or the developers will fail to gain rapport with the users, or people will fight interminably over meaningless methodological issues. (p. 88)

Because poor team skills waste so much company time, businesses are now putting pressure on educational institutions to provide authentic team experiences that will produce college graduates with strong interpersonal, management, and coauthoring skills. Instructors assign team projects to give students opportunities to develop these skills.

Second, instructors assign team projects so that students have opportunities to learn from their peers. Many students are motivated by collaborative learning. Co-writing and collaborating give students opportunities to share expertise, learn from others' mistakes as well as successes, and—most importantly—solidify what they have learned by teaching it to others.

Unfortunately, teams in school settings do not function just like teams in the workplace. Unlike school-based teams, work-based teams can develop longer histories of working together and are more likely to have clear-cut lines of authority. Thus, school-based teams have some unique challenges that are not present in work-based teams. This textbook attempts to teach you how to navigate some of these challenges using strategies that you can also carry into the workplace.

◆ Understanding Collaboration Methods

The three scenarios that begin this chapter illustrate some of the problems that arise when teams fail to fully plan out a project and agree on a collaboration method. In all three cases, the students being interviewed disagreed with their teammates over the specific steps the team needed to follow. These conflicting views of how the team should go about collaborating hurt the quality of the final projects and led to dissatisfaction with the team.

Understanding different collaboration methods and their respective costs and benefits can help teams identify and negotiate conflicting visions of how the group should proceed. When working on documents, groups can structure their collaboration using one of three basic methods (see Figure 1.1):

1. **Face-to-face.** The entire team sits down and writes the document together. Usually one or two team members sit at the computer and type while others give input.

2. **Divided.** The group breaks the document into sections and assigns each team member a section.

3. **Layered.** Each person on the team is assigned one or more specific roles. Each person works on the document in turn, adding his or her own expertise to the product. The document slowly accumulates in layers as each team member revises and improves upon what already exists.

The type of collaboration method a group uses has significant consequences for how the work proceeds. In the interviews beginning this chapter, Eduardo describes experiences typical of groups that rely on **divided** collaboration. Team members completed their individual sections at the last minute, there was no time for discussion of the final draft, and Eduardo is not sure if his teammates even read the final report. Moreover, one of the team members produced a section that was of particularly low quality—contributing to the disappointing grade this group received.

Whereas Eduardo's group never met to discuss the draft, Thomas's group tried to complete *all* of its work in team meetings. The team members' attempt to draft their entire proposal **face-to-face** not only was inefficient but also lowered project quality because they were rushed for time at the end and ended up dropping sections. In addition, although Thomas was not aware of it at the time, one of the group members was

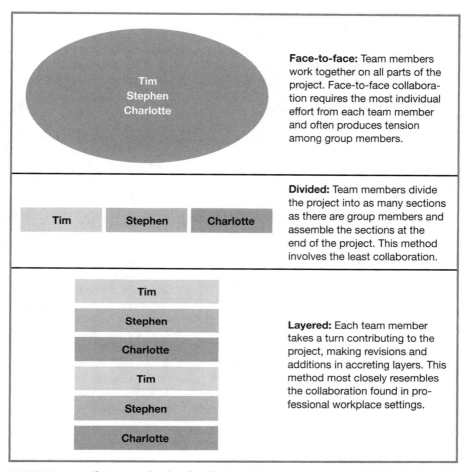

Face-to-face: Team members work together on all parts of the project. Face-to-face collaboration requires the most individual effort from each team member and often produces tension among group members.

Divided: Team members divide the project into as many sections as there are group members and assemble the sections at the end of the project. This method involves the least collaboration.

Layered: Each team member takes a turn contributing to the project, making revisions and additions in accreting layers. This method most closely resembles the collaboration found in professional workplace settings.

FIGURE 1.1. Three methods of collaboration

extremely upset with the group dynamics, perceiving the team as not valuing her input. When a team relies too much on face-to-face collaboration, such resentment is common because it is virtually impossible for three or more people sitting around a computer to contribute equally.

Susan's group illustrates how the failure to discuss a collaboration method as a group can produce conflict. Susan felt the group should have created the Web site face-to-face; however, Rene operated using a **layered** collaboration method in which she completed an initial draft and then tried to hand the project off to others to revise and finish. Although this layered approach seemed more appropriate to this project than Susan's face-to-face method, Rene's failure to discuss her collaboration plans resulted in a major breakdown in group dynamics.

See Table 1.1 for a summary of the advantages and drawbacks of the face-to-face, divided, and layered methods of collaboration.

Method	Advantages	Drawbacks
Face-to-face	• Allows team members to quickly share a large number of ideas—particularly useful for brainstorming and debating the pros and cons of different ideas. • Effective for drafting plans, outlines, and task schedules. • Effective for discussing graphic design, such as a company brochure or the layout of a Web page.	• Often difficult to schedule large blocks of time when the team can meet outside of class. • Can be difficult for everyone to have equal input—the person sitting at the keyboard can control what is said. • Ineffective for drafting text and content—wastes individual time and can produce conflict. • Often impossible in the workplace, where team members may be geographically distant.
Divided	• Allows the work to be completed in the least amount of time.	• Minimal collaboration. • Can be difficult to recover if one team member fails to do his or her share or does a poor job. • Content likely to contain duplications, gaps, and inconsistencies. • Style can suffer from inconsistent tone, word choice, and writing quality.
Layered	• Helps ensure a high-quality project because everyone has multiple opportunities to contribute, critique, and improve upon the project. • Maximizes the contributions of all group members. • Motivates the group because everyone feels ownership of the full document. • Particularly effective for drafting and revising. • Mirrors collaboration in the workplace.	• Different team members' roles may require unequal effort—this is common in a work setting but may create problems in a school setting, where all team members are expected to contribute equally. • Requires thoughtful planning up front—some team members may feel anxious spending time on planning rather than jumping into the details.

TABLE 1.1. Advantages and drawbacks of the three collaboration methods

Despite its substantial advantages, student teams tend to underutilize layered collaboration—probably because it requires the most planning and experience of the three methods. While face-to-face collaboration and divided collaboration seem to come naturally to student teams, layered collaboration requires forethought and some basic training to use it effectively. In part because layered collaboration is unfamiliar to students—and in part because it is the form of collaboration that most frequently leads to higher-quality products—this book stresses layered collaboration in much of the advice and many of the examples provided.

◆ Alternating Collaboration Methods

Often when students are assigned a team project, their first instinct is to schedule a series of face-to-face meetings. Not only does this put a tremendous strain on everyone's personal schedules, but face-to-face collaboration may not even be the most productive form of collaboration for the group at this stage. By figuring out which type of collaboration will be most beneficial at various stages in the project, team members can avoid many problems and ensure that they use their time together productively.

Few experienced teams rely exclusively on a single collaboration method. Most teams alternate collaboration methods throughout the project, depending on what the group is trying to accomplish at each stage. Thus, a team will often begin with face-to-face collaboration in the early stages of a project; switch to layered collaboration to complete the "heavy," detailed work of the project; and then switch back to face-to-face collaboration to discuss revisions or to work out a presentation. Or the team might initially divide up the work so that each team member drafts a section independently and then switch to layered collaboration for the revision process.

Table 1.2 illustrates a group that alternates the face-to-face and layered collaboration methods. In the early stages of the project, the group meets face-to-face to discuss the project's direction and to assign tasks to team members. About a third of the way through the project, the group switches to layered collaboration, with team members successively adding to, elaborating on, critiquing, and revising one another's work. Table 1.3 provides an overview of which types of collaboration are generally most effective at various stages of a project.

Switching collaboration methods might seem complicated at first. However, with a clearly defined **task schedule**, such as the one in Table 1.2, groups can easily stay on task. In fact, if you take away only one lesson from this book, it should be this: a well-planned task schedule is key to the success of any collaborative project. Task schedules will be discussed in more detail in the following chapters.

Deadline	Who	Task
3/02	Everyone	Initial group meeting
3/04	Everyone	Group meeting
3/04	Stephen	E-mail schedule and notes from group meeting
3/13	Tim	Complete client interviews; e-mail interview notes to the group
3/14	Everyone	Group meeting at 3:00 p.m. to discuss interviews
3/14	Stephen	E-mail notes from group meeting
3/21	Charlotte	E-mail rough draft of requirements document minus introduction and conclusion
3/23	Tim	E-mail comments on requirements document
3/29	Stephen	E-mail revised draft of requirements with introduction and conclusion added
3/31	Tim	E-mail draft of cover letter addressed to client
4/03	Charlotte	E-mail revised and polished draft of all materials to group for last-minute comments
4/04 a.m.	Stephen	E-mail editing suggestions to Charlotte
4/04 p.m.	Charlotte	Turn in final draft to professor by 3:00 p.m.

TABLE 1.2. Task schedule from a project that switches from face-to-face to layered collaboration
Tim is the researcher and client expert; Stephen is the project manager and secondary writer; Charlotte is the primary writer and editor. Note that the task schedule can be color-coded or shaded to highlight each team member's responsibilities.

Task or Project Stage	Most Appropriate Collaboration Method
Brainstorming	Face-to-face
Planning a task schedule	Face-to-face
Conducting research	Any, depending on the type of research
Drafting text	Layered or divided
Talking to third parties (instructors, clients, users)	Face-to-face or layered
Discussing a draft	Face-to-face or layered
Resolving disagreements or major changes to project	Face-to-face
Revising text	Layered
Preparing presentations or other visual materials	Layered or face-to-face
Editing text	Layered

TABLE 1.3. Most appropriate collaboration method for various stages of a project

Exercises

1. Think of a time when you were involved in a group project at school or at work. Which collaboration method or methods did your group use? How did your choice of collaboration methods contribute to the group's success? How did your choice of collaboration methods lead to conflicts, inefficiencies, or poor project quality? What would you do differently if you were to start this project from scratch?

> *The videos in this textbook are directly based on the interactions of actual students. Before you complete any of the video exercises, take a moment to watch the introductory video on the* Team Writing *Web site, which describes how the videos were produced and created.*

2. View Team Video 1: Mark, Natalie, and Keith on the *Team Writing* Web site. Answer the following questions about the video:

Team 1

   a. What method of collaboration does this team seem to be using?

   b. For each team member—Mark (typing at the computer), Natalie, and Keith—provide two or three words or short phrases describing their role on the team.

   c. Based on what you have observed, which team member do you think made the most important contribution, and which one made the least important contribution? Why?

   d. Review Table 1.1. Which drawbacks do you see illustrated in the way the students in this video are collaborating? What problems do you anticipate this team will have in the future if the students continue this style of collaboration?

   e. What changes would you suggest that this group make to improve their collaboration?

3. Once you have completed question 2, read Appendix C, "Responses and Outcomes for Team Video 1." Read about this project's outcome and what the team members themselves said when they viewed a copy of this video after the project was over.

   a. Now that you have more information, how would you modify your original responses to questions 2b–2e?

   b. What actions would you advise the unhappy members of this group to take? How would you have handled the situation if you were Natalie? If you were Mark?

   c. What major lessons can you learn from observing this team?

4. View Team Video 2: Shelly, Will, and Ben on the *Team Writing* Web site. Answer the following questions:

Team 2

a. What method of collaboration does this team seem to be using?

b. For each team member—Shelly, Will, and Ben—provide two or three words or short phrases describing their role on the team.

c. Review Table 1.1. Which drawbacks do you see illustrated in the way the students in this video are collaborating? What problems do you anticipate this team will have in the future if the students continue this style of collaboration?

d. What changes would you recommend that this team make to improve their collaboration?

e. What major lessons can you learn from observing this team?

Work Cited

DeMarco, T., & Lister, T. (1987). *Peopleware: Productive products and teams.* New York: Dorset House Publishing.

CHAPTER 2

Project Management

In a team evaluation at the end of his project, Ryan commented:

> Audrey was a great project manager. She really kept us on track. There were several times when I wasn't sure what I should do next. Then I just looked at her minutes and saw what it was I needed to finish up.

On another team, Bill similarly attributed team success to good project management:

> Steve did a great job keeping everybody updated. Because of him, everybody knew what their deadlines were and how the group was going. This was the first time I've been on a group project where everybody didn't wait until the last minute to throw everything together.

Project management is one of the least understood aspects of collaboration in student teams. Before we continue discussing how to organize a collaborative project, you should understand what project management involves and why a project manager is necessary—even on small projects.

◆ Why Do You Need a Project Manager?

Students frequently confuse the role of project manager with "boss," "leader," or even "dictator" and quite understandably decide that they do not want a project manager on their team. Instead of viewing the project manager as a kind of supervisor, think of the project manager as someone who plays a specific role on the team by keeping the project on course. The project manager's primary responsibility is to track the status of the project and to ensure that all team members know what they should be doing at any moment.

The larger and more complicated the team project is, the more important the role of project manager becomes. However, even small two-person projects can benefit from someone who acts as project manager by summarizing tasks and deadlines for the group. Often the project manager will do other work for the group; however, according to Charles Stratton, a technical writing consultant, even if he or she does nothing other than coordinate the team, the project manager "has earned his [or her] keep" (Stratton, 1989).

The project manager's specific duties include the following:

- Keeping the project on schedule by publicizing deadlines and responsibilities in the **task schedule**

- Holding people accountable by documenting action items in the **meeting minutes**

- Managing disagreements by documenting decisions in the meeting minutes

- Keeping team meetings on task by preparing **meeting agendas**

In addition, the project manager may, if needed, perform other tasks:

- Sending e-mail reminders of deadlines

- Notifying the instructor of problems, particularly missed deadlines

- Creating the initial **straw document** of the project

- Producing other documents related to the project, including **project plans**, **team charters**, and **progress reports**

On most projects, the manager will be doing work in addition to coordinating the project. Thus, a project manager might also double up as a co-writer, artist, or some other role on the team. However, on very large projects, it may be sufficient to have a project manager who does nothing other than manage the team.

The remainder of this chapter focuses on the three types of documents that are essential to good project management: task schedules, meeting minutes, and meeting agendas. This chapter also describes additional documents that the project manager should produce.

◆ Task Schedules: Publicizing Deadlines and Responsibilities

Once the team has brainstormed some initial ideas for the project and discussed how to organize the collaboration, the project manager needs to create a **written task schedule** that documents **deadlines**, **tasks**, and **responsibilities**. Such a document is absolutely essential to effective collaboration. (See Chapter 4, "Getting Started with the Task Schedule," for more details on how to develop and schedule a collaborative process.)

At a minimum, every project (even a two-person project) needs a task schedule that lists the three *W*s: *who* is responsible for doing *what* by *when*. This task schedule is continually updated as work is reassigned, new tasks are identified, or deadlines change. Table 2.1 shows a task schedule for a group collaborating on an instruction manual.

Each entry in a task schedule contains three vital pieces of information: a name, a deadline, and a brief description of the task. A good task schedule should also build in **padding**—additional downtime between major steps that allows the group to recover in case a particular step takes longer than expected. For instance, this group has built in two days of padding between 9/12 (the date that everyone's drafts or tasks are due) and 9/14 (the date that the usability tests are scheduled). Similar padding is built into the schedule between 9/19 (the date that Amy will compile and edit a completed manual) and 9/21 (the date the manual is due). This padding allows the group to stay on schedule even if one or more of the major parts of the project are unexpectedly delayed.

To be effective, a task schedule needs to be visible. Thus, the project manager must *distribute the schedule to the entire group* (usually through e-mail) each time it is updated. In addition, it is a good idea to keep a copy of the task schedule in a centralized document server that the entire

Deadline	Who	Task	Status
9/04	Amy	Write topic proposal and bring to group meeting	Completed
9/04	Everyone	Review and discuss topic proposal at in-class meeting	Completed
9/06	Amy	Turn in revised topic proposal to instructor	Completed
9/09	Jessica	Bring template with sample layout for manual to meeting	
9/09	Everyone	Discuss and revise template at in-class meeting	
9/12	Bryan	Write instructions for installing motor and arms; e-mail	
9/12	Jessica	Write instructions for assembling base; e-mail	
9/12	Amy	Line up two users for 9/14; prepare all materials for usability tests; e-mail group with status	
9/14	Everyone	Test-drive instructions with users at 3:00 p.m. in the library	
9/14	Amy	E-mail a list of changes to group	
9/17	Bryan and Jessica	Revise instructions; e-mail Amy	
9/19	Amy	Edit manual; prepare overview and table of contents; compile and e-mail completed manual to group	
9/21	Everyone	Group meeting at 3:00 p.m. to review final draft; turn in draft	

TABLE 2.1. Task schedule for a three-person group working on an instruction manual

team can access. The project manager may also want to e-mail a copy of the team's initial task schedule to the instructor so that he or she has a copy in case the group has problems with an individual team member later in the project.

The task schedule in Table 2.1 reflects a layered collaboration model. Each team member has his or her own set of responsibilities but also has opportunities to comment and improve on work created by others. A task schedule is essential for implementing a layered collaboration. Such a carefully structured and planned project has a high potential for success.

Dangers of Operating without a Task Schedule

The need for a task schedule should be obvious; nonetheless, many student teams try to operate without one. Without a task schedule, teams are likely to:

- **Miss deadlines.**

- **Duplicate effort.** Two people may complete the same task because neither one is aware that another teammate has been assigned to do it.

- **Procrastinate.** Without a specific deadline in writing, team members might put off their parts of the project until the last minute, thus ensuring a sloppy, uncoordinated project.

- **Encourage slackers.** Some team members will avoid doing any work on the project at all. They may claim that they didn't know a deliverable was due or that they thought someone else was planning to do it. A clear task schedule eliminates these excuses and holds that person responsible for completing a fair share of the work.

Finally, without a clear task schedule that has been circulated via e-mail and/or stored in a centralized group space, teams have no way to appeal to the instructor if someone on the team fails to do his or her work. Without written documentation, the instructor has to take the word of the complaining student. A written task schedule gives the instructor a resource that he or she can use to implement penalties and reassign work.

◆ Meeting Minutes: Building Accountability and Consensus

The following conversation illustrates a common misconception that students often have about meeting minutes:

> **Interviewer:** *Now, I noticed that in team meetings you frequently took notes. What was in those notes?*

Jessica: *I have them right here. . . . Here's some, showing what every-body had to do.*

Interviewer: *Okay. So when you took notes, it was along the lines of what different people had to do?*

Jessica: *Exactly.*

Interviewer: *Did you ever e-mail notes out to group members? Or just say this is a reminder of what we did or what we decided on?*

Jessica: *No, I didn't, but that's a good idea. I think they all saw me write, I think. Maybe I thought they were writing them down too, so they may have them.*

Interviewer: *Yeah, but different people could have been writing down different things.*

Jessica (surprised): *That's true. I didn't think of that.*

Many teams confuse meeting minutes with individual note taking — or with secretarial work that simply records everything that happened during a meeting. In fact, meeting minutes are managerial documents that direct the project by deciding what information is important enough to include and what needs to happen next. Good meeting minutes help the team come to a consensus on the project's progress, who is responsible for what, and where the team needs to go next.

Good meeting minutes contain the following (see Figure 2.1):

- **Action items.** This is a "to do" list that details who needs to do which tasks. Whenever someone on the team volunteers for a task — or whenever the entire team is given a task — this information needs to be recorded.

- **Decisions.** The minutes should include a brief record of important decisions made during the meeting.

- **Next steps.** The minutes should record the questions or actions that will be taken up at the next meeting.

- **Attendance.** The names of people who attended the meeting should be listed so that the team has a record of who is contributing and who has agreed to team decisions.

In addition, meeting minutes **must be distributed to the entire team soon after the meeting**, usually within 24 hours. The minutes are useless if team members do not have them in their hands to refer to. If a team does not have time to distribute minutes after a meeting, then it didn't have time for the meeting itself.

Randall Walker, an industrial engineer with 15 years of management experience in the military, explains that minutes are essential:

> You can say one thing to five people and they will interpret it five different ways. It's critical to put team decisions in writing because at least it gives them an opportunity to say "No, that's not the context of what I said," or

"That's not the way I interpreted what we agreed upon." If you don't have it documented, it's he said/she said three weeks [later]. . . . So I think documentation of those encounters [is] absolutely critical in moving forward; otherwise you take one step forward and four steps back and one step forward and four steps back, and you can only take so many steps back before you drop off the cliff.

Library Project Meeting Minutes
April 8, 2008

Attendance: Alex, Alicia, Sefu (Phil absent because of emergency dental visit)

Action items:
Alex: Double-check room availability and send out confirmation to users
Alicia: E-mail draft of usability script to group by Wednesday night
Sefu: Make changes to artwork and send to Phil by Wednesday night
Phil: Implement changes to home page and insert new artwork by class on Thursday

Discussion:

- Mapped out the details of the usability tests
  - Usability tests will be held in LL15 next Friday from 12:00 to 3:00 p.m. Alex will double-check room availability and send confirmation e-mail to users.
  - Alex will bring his video camera to record the tests.
  - Roles: Alicia will be the moderator for all three tests. Alex will record. Sefu and Phil will take observational notes.
- Discussed changes to the artwork
  - The home page logo/image is taking up too much space. It needs to be cropped or resized.
  - The photo of the computer lab on the "Student Resources" page is too dark. It looks depressing.
- Discussed changes to the home page
  - Main navigation links should be reordered: "Search Catalog" should be first, followed by "Search Journals," "Hours," "Resources," and finally "Contact Information."
  - Link to "Hours" is broken.
  - A copyright logo should be placed in the footer.
- Discussed what we want to get out of the usability tests next Friday
  - What do users think of the artwork? (Maybe have some alternative designs to show them?)
  - Does the order of navigational elements make sense?
  - Are there any broken links?
  - Can users find basic information (such as circulation hours, lab hours, phone numbers) without help?
  - Can users find all journal and book search features without help?

Next steps: Next meeting in class on Thursday, April 10. Need to go over changes to artwork, search for broken links, and take a look at the usability script.

FIGURE 2.1. Meeting minutes
These minutes contain action items, major decisions, next steps, and attendance. The minutes should be circulated to the team within 24 hours of the meeting.

Andrew Grove, the CEO of Intel, a major computer chip manufacturer, agrees:

> If a meeting was worth calling in the first place, the effort to produce and distribute the minutes is a small additional investment necessary to realize its full benefits. (Grove, 1995)

The most important information in the minutes is the list of action items detailing who will do what. Ken West, an operations research manager with more than 10 years' experience supervising teams, clarifies:

> Even if you don't produce formal minutes, at the end of the meeting, there should be a page that says you're going to do this, you're going do this, you're going do this, and you're going to do this. The person who is the project manager better make sure that that's written down. It's their responsibility to follow up that things get done.

Dangers of Operating without Meeting Minutes

As the previous quotes from managers testify, meeting minutes are essential to the forward progress of a team. Without a central set of minutes, teams will

- **Waste time.** Without minutes, teams will revisit issues that have already been decided, repeat information that has already been shared, or rehash conversations that have already been completed. Moreover, the minutes allow teams to pick up the next meeting right where they left off.

- **Proceed without consensus.** As Randall Walker stated, you can say something to five people and they will interpret it five different ways. The minutes provide a centralized interpretation of the team's decisions and ensure that everyone is "on the same page."

- **Forget important details.** The minutes serve as a reminder of important material that the team has discussed. Without minutes, teams will almost certainly forget some of this material.

- **Encourage slackers.** The minutes publicize the commitments each person has made and put pressure on everyone to perform up to the team's standards.

◆ Meeting Agenda: Keeping Discussions on Track

A meeting agenda is a *brief* list of topics to be discussed at the meeting. This list of topics does not need to be comprehensive—in other words, the team can discuss items not on the agenda; however, an agenda helps

TO: Team
FR: Jason
Subject: Agenda for meeting on 3/7, 1:00 p.m., Miller Tech

Hi Team:

We are meeting at 1:00 p.m. on Thursday, 3/7, in the Miller Tech computer lab.

Agenda:
* Confirm meeting time with instructor
* Discuss Karen's revisions (see attachment Karen e-mailed earlier today)
* Report from Susan detailing her research on costs

Let me know if there is anything else that you think should go on the agenda.

FIGURE 2.2. Meeting agenda sent via e-mail
The agenda contains a short list of items to be discussed, along with a reminder of the meeting time and location. An agenda must be distributed to the team in advance of the meeting.

ensure that nothing important gets left out of the discussion. When people who are not part of the team attend a meeting, a brief agenda is particularly important because it lets them know what to expect and allows them to prepare for questions team members might ask.

To allow people time to prepare for the meeting, an agenda should be distributed **in advance of the meeting** (see Figure 2.2).

Dangers of Operating without a Meeting Agenda

A meeting agenda is essential to make sure that the team meeting is really needed and that the team stays on track. Without a clear agenda, teams will

* **Manage their time poorly.** A written agenda allows a team to jump directly to what needs to be accomplished without wasting time figuring out what needs to be discussed. Moreover, without an agenda, the team might overlook important items, thus necessitating another meeting.

* **Show up unprepared.** The agenda gives everyone a chance to think about the items that will be discussed at the meeting, to do any necessary research, and to prepare any information or material that needs to be distributed.

* **Hold unnecessary meetings.** Sometimes, the project manager will begin to prepare a meeting agenda only to realize that there are no issues for the team to discuss. In this case, after checking with the rest of the team, the project manager may cancel the meeting.

◆ E-mail Reminders and Notifications: Stepping In When Problems Occur

The project manager is always focused on the future direction of the group. Even meeting minutes, which at first might seem just to be records of past actions, are produced in order to shape the group's future direction and ensure that everyone follows through on commitments made during the meeting.

In the unfortunate event that some teammates are negligent in performing their duties or a project goes off schedule, the project manager needs to continue this focus on the team's future. Thus, when a project manager steps in to take action on missed deadlines, missed meetings, or unacceptable work, his or her focus needs to be on finding a solution rather than spreading blame.

How forcefully the project manager steps in depends on the situation and the severity of the offense. Usually, small problems can be handled through gentle reminder e-mails. Larger problems that threaten the project's success may require contacting the instructor.

For instance, a project manager should always send a "gentle" reminder to a teammate immediately after a deadline has passed. Figure 2.3 illustrates a gentle reminder sent directly to a teammate who has missed a deadline. This reminder assumes that Susan plans on completing the work but either has encountered unexpected difficulties or has had some personal emergency that has prevented her from completing the work on time. The e-mail focuses on highlighting the effects that this lateness might have on the team's future schedule.

The next step up in severity occurs when a teammate is several days behind schedule, has missed deadlines in the past, or has otherwise shown

---

TO: Susan
FR: Jason
Subject: Draft due date

Dear Susan:

Just a reminder that your draft was due to the team by 5:00 p.m. yesterday. Do you think you can get it out by Wednesday morning? If there is some problem, please let me know ASAP so that I can revise the task schedule.

Thanks,
Jason

FIGURE 2.3. A gentle reminder that a deadline has passed
Such reminders should be sent (usually directly to the person involved) the first time a team member has missed a deadline.

> TO: Susan
> FR: Jason
> Subject: Draft due date — second notice
>
> Dear Susan:
>
> Your draft was due more than two days ago, and we haven't heard anything from you.
> Karen needs your materials so that she can compile everything and make revisions by
> Friday. If you cannot get the materials to us today, please let us know because Karen
> will have to rearrange her schedule in order to get everything done. I apologize if you
> are experiencing some crisis. We are starting to get worried about meeting the deadline
> and will have to contact the instructor if we don't hear from you. Please let us know
> what to expect.
>
> Thanks,
> Jason

FIGURE 2.4. A more pointed reminder that a deadline has passed
Such reminders should point out the effects that a teammate's delays or poor
performance will have on the rest of the team.

himself or herself deserving of a more pointed reminder. This reminder
should gently point out the consequences that the teammate's actions
have on the rest of the team. The project manager may want to copy the
entire team in the "cc" section of the e-mail. Figure 2.4 illustrates a
pointed reminder.

If a teammate does not respond appropriately to this pointed reminder,
the project manager might want to send an e-mail to the instructor, if for
no other reason than to document the team's problems. Figure 2.5 illustrates an e-mail notifying the instructor about a problem.

Chapter 8, "Troubleshooting Team Problems," provides additional
advice on handling problematic teammates.

◆ Other Documents the Project Manager May Produce

Task schedules, meeting minutes, and meeting agendas should be produced for any project, no matter how large or small. These documents
are essential to keeping the team on task. Projects that neglect these are
destined for trouble and unproductive conflict. However, larger projects
may require additional routine maintenance documents with which the
project manager keeps the team on track. (See Table 2.2.)

TO: Professor Williams
FR: Jason Carpenter
CC: Carrie S., Matt B.
Subject: Question about a team problem

Dear Professor Williams:

My team would like to notify you and ask your advice about a problem we are having. I have attached a copy of our task schedule. As you can see, a draft of the cost-benefit analysis was due on Monday. I received a brief outline from Susan (the person responsible) on Wednesday night. Not only was this two days late, but it was not what the team needed. It is now Thursday, and the next leg of the project is about to be officially behind schedule.

Since the cost information is key to our proposal, we are unsure how to proceed. Should we give Susan another chance, or should we assign this task to someone else and basically cut her out of the project? Any advice or assistance you can provide would be greatly appreciated.

Thank you very much for your help.
Jason Carpenter

FIGURE 2.5. E-mail notifying the instructor about a problem
Although the e-mail documents the group's past problems, the overall tone and direction of the e-mail focuses on finding a future solution. Jason asks the instructor for advice rather than a solution to the group's problems. Even if the instructor does not take any action, such an e-mail provides documentation of the team's problems and can protect responsible team members if any grading disputes come up in the future.

◆ Starting the Process with a Straw Document

A "straw" document is an excellent way to start a group writing project that is taking on a complex task for which no clear format exists. A straw document is basically an extremely rough skeleton of the project that the writer expects to be blown down, like a straw house. The purpose of the straw document is to draw the team into a discussion of the pros and cons of various directions the project might take. In this way, the straw document is a tool to facilitate group brainstorming about specific details.

With a straw document, the project manager brings in a very flimsy but relatively complete draft of the entire document or document section. The straw document should contain a comprehensive list of topics or points the document needs to address, but the details do not have to be fully fleshed out. The goal is to have *something* down on paper so

Document	Description
Team charter	An internal document (one that is not shared with others outside of the team) that describes the "big picture" goals and priorities of the project. Teams rely on the team charter to help resolve conceptual conflicts that occur as the project progresses. The team charter is particularly helpful for teams that have not worked together before or for large-scale projects. Chapter 3, "Getting Started with the Team Charter," describes this document in more detail.
Project plan	A formal document describing the scope of the work for an external audience, which may include instructors, supervisors, or clients. The project plan is used to assure outside stakeholders that the team is headed down the right path. Instructors generally review project plans to make sure that teams have picked projects that meet the assignment guidelines and can be accomplished within the allotted time frame.
	Most project plans contain the following information: (1) what problem the project is addressing; (2) what work is to be done; (3) what major deliverables will be produced; (4) who will be involved and what their responsibilities will be; (5) what major deadlines or milestones will be met.
	Most workplaces have their own unofficial guidelines for project plans. If you are required to complete a project plan, ask your instructor or supervisor for a model you can follow.
Progress report	Usually an informal document that gives an instructor, supervisor, or client information on the team's progress on a project over a set period of time. This document is used primarily for projects that take at least three months to complete.
	Progress reports contain the following information: (1) how much of the work is complete; (2) what the team is currently working on; (3) what work remains to be done; (4) what problems have arisen; (5) how the project is going in general (whether the project is on schedule).
	There are innumerable variations in the format of a progress report. If you are required to file a progress report, ask your instructor or supervisor for a model you can follow.

TABLE 2.2. Additional documents a project manager may need to produce

that the team can begin to discuss the drawbacks and benefits of various alternatives.

Because of the nature of straw documents, they are used only in the very beginning stages of writing. The writer of the straw document must be ready to stand back and not become upset when others eventually knock down parts of the document. One engineer with extensive experience working on major proposals clarifies this point:

An important point when you put a straw [document] up is that people mustn't be offended if other people criticize it, tear it apart, offer constructive criticism. You've got to take it in the light that different people have different opinions. It saves a lot of time. If you hadn't written it down [as a straw document,] they wouldn't have thought about it. (Sales, 2006)

Another engineer at the same company states that the great advantage of the straw document is that "it doesn't matter if you get it wrong. In fact, you expect to get it wrong, so you can rush it out any old how. It is safe to do so because you know it will be sorted out later" (Sales, 2006).

Sometimes, groups can benefit from looking at several different straw drafts. This is often the case when there is serious disagreement about how to proceed. In this situation, one or two team members prepare multiple drafts for the group to compare and contrast.

When working with a straw document, everyone in the group needs to understand that it is intended to be a temporary document that will likely be completely rewritten later. It should not be confused with a complete draft of the document (see Chapter 6, "Revising with Others," for information on working with more complete drafts). In other words, the straw document should be used to spark discussions about big, conceptual issues—and not issues such as word choice, formatting, or even the details of much of the content, all of which are more appropriately discussed at the rough-draft stage of the project.

Exercises

1. Review the three scenarios at the beginning of Chapter 1, "Planning Your Collaboration." How might each of these groups' problems have been alleviated with a task schedule?

2. Think of a time when you were involved in a group project. Did this project have a project manager? If so, was this person effective? If you had had the type of project manager described in this chapter, how might any problems that your group experienced have been prevented?

3. Read Appendix B, "Sample Meeting Minutes," which contains three versions of the meeting minutes from one four-person team. All three versions contain the same information. Which version do you think will be the most effective for keeping the team on track? Why?

The videos in this textbook are directly based on the interactions of actual student teams. Before you complete any of the video exercises, take a moment to watch the introductory video on the Team Writing Web site, which describes how the videos were produced and created.

4. View Team Video 3: Jamaal, Jim, Don, and Tonya on the *Team Writing* Web site. This group of students is preparing a proposal to irrigate a third-world country. To the best of your ability based on the information you have, create a brief set of meeting minutes to follow up this group's discussion. What important information has this group failed to discuss? What issues does this team need to take up at its next meeting?

Team 3

5. What collaboration method does the team in this video seem to be using? What problems do you anticipate if the team continues to collaborate using this method?

Works Cited

Grove, A. (1995). *High output management.* New York: Vintage Books.

Sales, H. E. (2006). *Professional communication in engineering.* New York: Palgrave Macmillan.

Stratton, C. R. (1989). Collaborative writing in the workplace. *IEEE Transactions on Professional Communication, 32*(3), 178–182.

CHAPTER 3

Getting Started with the Team Charter

Kelly and Sean were both members of a four-person team working on a Web site. They made the following observations:

Kelly: *Sean has done nothing. We asked him to do the first draft of the project proposal by compiling all of our information into a paper. Instead, he came up with less than one page that didn't meet the requirements of the proposal at all. This is really pitiful since we gave him over four pages of our own work to build on. Also, he was supposed to add what research he had done to the proposal, and there was no mention of it, so I'm assuming that he hasn't done any research. We ended up using the research that Eli got from his interview. Sean has showed up to every meeting; however, he has added nothing during any of the meetings. In fact, during the last meeting, he was chatting on Instant Messenger on his laptop while we were all discussing and working on the project proposal. . . . In the last week, he has finally shown some interest in helping out, but I'm reluctant in giving him anything important to do as he has so far proven himself unreliable.*

Sean: *I haven't spent much time at all on the project, sadly. As far as I'm aware, Kelly is the only one who's done much the last two weeks, though I could be wrong—it wouldn't be the first time I've missed something obvious during this project. . . . The rest of the team seems to work together excellently, but I've felt ignored a few times. I completely missed part of the requirement of the proposal, and instead of saying anything to me, Eli and Angela just completely rewrote it. I've also felt ignored during meetings and thus have been mostly silent during group reviews of papers, which would ordinarily be my strongest moments. . . . Everything that I've done so far on the project has been incredibly subpar by my own standards. I've done two writing assignments, and both times, I only noticed a fraction of the instructions we were given. . . . Much*

27

of the time I felt confused as to what was going on. This was my own fault—for the first few weeks of the project, I was highly unmotivated. At the time I'm writing this, though, I think I'm about to be given some content to make a page for, so that's not as bad as it could be.

Before you continue reading, take a moment to think about what this team could have done to prevent the problems that it experienced. How would you characterize the problems with this team?

◆ The Team Charter: An Ounce of Prevention Is Worth a Pound of Cure

At the start of a project, the team is usually eager to charge ahead and start productive work right away. However, teams do well to bear in mind the slogan "Failing to plan is planning to fail." A team that spends an hour at the very beginning of the project discussing goals, expectations, and team norms can save substantial time and stress later on in the project.

Many experienced practitioners in a range of fields recommend that teams develop a **team charter** in the first meetings. A team charter is a brief, informal document that describes the "big picture" goals and priorities of the project. The official purpose of a team charter is to have a written statement of the team's priorities and norms that the team can use to resolve any problems or confusion that may occur later in the project. The unofficial purpose, particularly when team members have not worked together before, is to air any differences that they might have in goals, expectations, and commitment levels *before* the project begins.

For instance, if your project involves a client outside of the classroom, you may find that some team members put a priority on meeting the client's expectations, whereas others prioritize according to the instructor's exact directions. Similarly, you may find that team members have different ideas about the effort they are willing to invest in the project. It is better to know about these differences up front rather than discover them later on.

In general, the bigger the project, the more important the team charter is. Team charters differ greatly in content and format depending on the type of organization and project. For student projects, an effective team charter should contain the following information:

1. Overall, broad team goals for the project

2. Measurable, specific team goals

3. Personal goals

4. Individual level of commitment to the project

5. Other information about team members that may affect the project

6. Statement of how the team will resolve impasses

7. Statement of how the team will handle missed deadlines

8. Statement of what constitutes unacceptable work and how the team will handle this

Because the team charter is an internal document (something that will be seen only within the team) and because the real point of a team charter lies in discussing it rather than in writing it, this document can be composed in a face-to-face setting. The goal of the team charter is to uncover and discuss potential problems in a low-key setting, before any work has been assigned.

This chapter discusses what goes into a team charter. Before you start working on the charter with your group, take a moment to honestly assess your background, goals, and preparation for this project by completing the team preparation worksheet in Figure 3.1. (You can also download a copy of this worksheet from the *Team Writing* Web site at <bedfordstmartins.com/teamwriting>.)

◆ Team Goals: What Constitutes Success?

Your first action as a team should be to agree on what defines a successful project. Spend a few minutes discussing the one or two top broad goals you have for the project. Examples of broad goals include:

- Making an original argument

- Presenting our data accurately and effectively

- Persuading the audience to accept our solution

- Following the format and guidelines of the assignment sheet precisely

- Designing a product that satisfies the client

- Creating instructions that a computer novice can follow without mistakes

Do *not* simply list "getting an A" as one of your priorities. Instead, try to break down what criteria are most important to meet in order to receive an A. It may be that one person believes that getting an A means satisfying the client while another team member believes it means finding an original solution to a problem (whether or not the client wants an original solution). Again, the goal here is to uncover any fundamental differences about what the team is trying to accomplish before you start.

Team Preparation Worksheet

1. What strengths do you have relative to this project? (Check all that apply.)
   - ☐ Above-average writing ability
   - ☐ Above-average information-finding/research skills
   - ☐ Above-average computing skills
   - ☐ Above-average visual design/graphic design skills
   - ☐ Above-average leadership or management skills
   - ☐ Other (Describe): _____

2. What would you most like to learn from this project? (Check all that apply.)
   - ☐ Improve writing speed
   - ☐ Improve writing skills
   - ☐ Improve editing skills
   - ☐ Improve research skills
   - ☐ Improve data analysis skills
   - ☐ Improve PowerPoint skills
   - ☐ Improve other computer skills
   - ☐ Improve visual design skills
   - ☐ Improve management skills
   - ☐ Other (Describe): _____

3. What is your level of commitment to the project? (Check the one that best applies.)
   - ☐ I plan to get an A on this project and will make whatever sacrifices are necessary.
   - ☐ I want an A but am limited in the time/effort I can dedicate to the project.
   - ☐ I will be satisfied with a B on this project.
   - ☐ My goal is simply to receive a passing grade on this project.

4. What scheduling issues or other commitments do you have that might interfere with this project?

5. What concerns do you have about your skills or abilities that might affect how your team views your performance on this project?

6. Would you like to negotiate an agreement with the team that assigns you less responsibility for the project in exchange for a lower grade?

7. In your opinion, what does this team have to accomplish to make this project a success?

FIGURE 3.1. Team Preparation Worksheet

You can also download a copy of this worksheet from the *Team Writing* Web site at <bedfordstmartins.com/teamwriting>.

◆ Measurable Goals: How Can You Measure Success?

After your team has set out goals about what defines success, you need to translate your broad goals into measurable goals with objective, specific criteria that are clearly either met or not met. Creating measurable goals is an essential step in workplace teams, which might come up with goals such as *increasing productivity by 20 percent* or *reducing accidents by at least 40 percent*. These goals are specific, objective, and measurable: they can be listed as numbers, so there should be little disagreement over whether or not they are met. Student teams may have more difficulty in generating measurable goals because projects are smaller and fewer external, objective measures are available. Nevertheless, creating measurable goals is an important skill that you should begin to practice now.

Examples of measurable goals include:

- Meeting all 10 of the assignment sheet's guidelines for the report's format

- Meeting or beating all the deadlines set out in the task schedule

- Reducing the word count by 15 percent between the rough draft and the final draft by eliminating wordiness and repetitiveness without deleting any content

- Writing instructions clearly enough that novice users voice no more than two questions or instances of confusion during usability testing

- Creating a Web site that four out of five classmates rank as user-friendly in anonymous surveys

- Citing at least four sources in the works cited page

- Having fewer than one grammatical error or typo per page

Although "getting an A" is a measurable goal, it is not a useful one because the team will not know whether this goal has been achieved until after the project has been completed, at which point it is too late to act on this goal. Instead, try to define measurable goals that can serve as a checklist before turning in the project.

◆ Personal Goals: What Do Team Members Want Out of the Project?

Next, try to uncover what is most important to each member of the team. Examples of personal goals are:

- Improving my writing skills

- Learning how to create a visually compelling PowerPoint presentation

- Creating a document that I can talk about on job interviews

- Having a productive and friendly team experience

- Completing the project with as little effort as possible

This last goal will almost certainly bring you into conflict with other team members, who will understandably wonder if they can trust you. However, there is some benefit to acknowledging this up front in order to avoid becoming a **negative contributor** (see the section "Negative Contributors").

Understanding what each team member hopes to gain personally from the project will help the group in the next step of defining and assigning roles and tasks. These statements of personal investment in the project should also help the group to determine specific directions for the project.

◆ Individual Commitment: How Much Effort Will Each Person Invest?

In addition to discussing project goals, team members should also discuss their degree of commitment to these goals. Do different team members have different ideas about the amount of time and effort that is needed to succeed? Is everyone truly willing to invest the effort needed to get a good grade on the project? Does everybody feel equally strongly about the importance of getting an A?

Many texts on teamwork assume that everyone on the project will have total commitment to the project—or else can be motivated to contribute 100 percent with just a little prodding. However, in reality, team members have responsibilities outside of the project and different levels of commitment and internal motivation. By frankly discussing what each person is able or willing to contribute up front, teams can anticipate and avoid potential problems.

The team has some concrete options for dealing with team members who have low commitment levels:

1. Team members with low commitment can be **assigned fewer or less critical tasks** on the project so that if they do not follow through, other team members can pick up the slack.

2. The team can consider formalizing an arrangement in which **one team member negotiates to do less work in exchange for a lower grade**. For instance, the team charter might state that John Doe will contribute approximately 25 percent less work than other

team members and consequently will receive a one-letter grade reduction on the project. (Check with your instructor to see if this is an option.)

Simply knowing that a particular team member has low motivation can often protect the team against surprises and extreme resentment later on in the project.

Situations in which team members contribute unequal amounts of effort mirror conditions that you might find in the workplace. In work-based teams, one or two team members often may be committed full-time to a project while others have other work priorities and contribute at a much lower level.

◆ Other Information: What Other Factors Might Affect Performance?

Do you have a personal commitment that will make you unavailable during a particular time frame? Do you have a pending personal emergency that may make you less dependable than you are normally? Are you worried that you will have difficulty meeting your team's expectations for the quality of the work? You should express these concerns and potential limitations at the beginning of the project so that you don't become a **negative contributor** to the group—someone whose presence hurts the team more than it helps.

If the team knows about shortcomings or potential obstacles up front, it can work these constraints into the task schedule. For instance, Cynthia was asked to draft a proposal but had little experience with this type of writing. The team responded by scheduling an extra round of early feedback so that Cynthia could be sure she was going in the right direction. Similarly, Jiang was worried that his poor English skills might hurt the team. The team was able to plan for this by scheduling additional time for Jiang to visit the school's writing center and receive feedback on his grammar before submitting his material to the group.

By understanding your needs and preferences before you start working on a team, you can recognize when your roles and responsibilities on the team are in conflict with your individual needs. Learning to recognize those conflicts and to positively address them represents one of the strongest opportunities for growth that people receive from working in teams.

Negative Contributors

> **Chris:** *I think everyone noticed that Stephanie felt like an outsider within the group. This is entirely her fault. If Stephanie would have attended class like she said she would, then we wouldn't have a problem with her feeling left out. . . . Our presentation is only five days away. Stephanie doesn't have a freakin' clue what is going*

on. . . . I don't know what she feels she is contributing, but it isn't that much.

Stephanie is a negative contributor because rather than helping her team finish the project, she has created an additional problem for her teammates to solve. Similarly, Sean (described at the beginning of this chapter) is also a negative contributor. Negative contributors include those who miss deadlines or meetings, turn in substandard work, or engage in unproductive conflict that does not further group goals.

Groups do have options for handling negative contributors: they can be *removed from the team* by the instructor, or they can receive poor evaluations from their teammates at the end of the project that translate into a *lowered project grade*. Of course, these are worst-case scenarios—if possible, it is better to prevent these negative scenarios from occurring.

The best way to avoid becoming a negative contributor is to be honest about your skills and commitments at the beginning of the project. For instance, if you know you will be able to dedicate only a limited number of hours a week or that your skills in a particular area are weak, tell the team about these constraints up front. The team can then factor these constraints into the task schedule. Similarly, if the team knows that you are inexperienced with a particular technology needed for the project, such as FrontPage, someone more experienced can be assigned as your "backup" in case you need to ask for help.

A good, clear task schedule with plenty of overlapping responsibilities and "padding" (extra space in the project for missed deadlines or emergencies) can help prevent any problems that negative contributors might cause. The clear task schedule lets team members know immediately when a task has not been completed, and the padding gives the team a chance to recover in a worst-case scenario.

◆ Irreconcilable Differences: How Will the Team Resolve Impasses?

Chapter 5, "Constructive Conflict," discusses the benefits of constructive conflict and why teams benefit from the healthy debate of ideas. However, there will be times when teams are unable to resolve their disagreements. A team charter that details when and how the team will handle impasses, or stalemates, will help the team progress even in the face of disagreement. The team charter should contain a brief one- or two-sentence statement of how the team will resolve continuing disagreements and at what point (two meetings, 30 minutes of discussion) the team will pursue the resolution method. Table 3.1 describes the four basic methods for resolving impasses and their advantages and disadvantages.

Method	Advantages	Disadvantages
Consensus: Discuss the issue until everyone agrees.	• The team will reach the best possible compromise.	• The process is time-consuming. • The consensus may be "fake"—someone on the team may give in just so that the team can move on.
Majority rules: Vote and adopt the majority decision.	• The impasse is resolved quickly. • The solution does not involve anyone outside the team.	• Some team members may feel left out or that others are "ganging up" on them.
Instructor decides: Present both sides anonymously to the instructor and let him or her decide.	• Feelings are unlikely to be hurt. • The team will have more information about what the instructor wants.	• It takes time to contact the instructor and present both sides. • The instructor may not want to intervene.
Third party decides: Present both sides anonymously to a classmate, a client (if applicable), or another party and ask that person to decide.	• Feelings are unlikely to be hurt.	• It may take time to contact a third party and present the information.

TABLE 3.1. Four methods for resolving impasses

◆ Late Work: How Will the Team Handle Missed Deadlines?

Missed deadlines signal a lack of commitment and a breach of trust. Team members rely on one another to make commitments; if a team member fails to honor a commitment, other group members will assume that the person is not trustworthy.

Teams should decide in advance how they will handle missed deadlines. Having procedures in place helps prevent the situation because team members will know there are clear consequences to their actions and also helps defuse the situation if it does occur.

The team charter should spell out how to handle missed deadlines. The following examples show some typical wording:

- The project manager e-mails a reminder to the team member who is late. If the team member does not respond within 24 hours, the project manager contacts the instructor. If the team member does respond with a valid excuse and a reasonable deadline, the project manager informs the rest of the team of the new deadline.

- The project manager e-mails a reminder to the team member who is late. If the team member does not submit acceptable work within 24 hours of this e-mail, the project manager contacts the rest of the team, explaining the situation and asking for input on how to proceed.

See Chapter 8, "Troubleshooting Team Problems," for more information on dealing with tardiness.

◆ Unacceptable Work: How Will the Team Handle Poor-Quality Contributions?

Sometimes, team members meet deadlines but submit work that is clearly unacceptable because it lacks important required information, falls considerably short of the page requirements, is riddled with grammatical errors, or has other shortcomings. Dealing with unacceptable work is often more stressful for the team than coping with missed deadlines because deciding what is unacceptable requires judgment and sometimes awkward discussions.

The team charter should list some **general criteria for unacceptable work** (for example, rough drafts missing more than 25 percent of the required information; near-final drafts that do not meet all of the assignment criteria), a **plan for notifying** a team member that the work is unacceptable, and a **recommended deadline** for revising unacceptable work. Criteria for unacceptable work should distinguish between rough drafts that the team will subsequently revise and more finished work produced closer to the final project deadline. Table 3.2 lists some ways of handling unacceptable work, along with their advantages and disadvantages.

◆ Putting It All Together

A team charter not only helps the team plan for negative situations but also prevents these situations from occurring in the first place because team members (1) have a nonthreatening place to **voice concerns** about the project and (2) are aware that there are **clear consequences** for letting the team down. A calm discussion about how the team will handle

Method	Advantages	Disadvantages
Project manager says nothing: Project manager asks another team member to rewrite a section (or does it himself or herself) and says nothing to the person directly.	• Avoids an unpleasant conversation • Resolves the issue quickly • May be appropriate if the final deadline is approaching and/or this is not the first time this person has produced unacceptable work	• May be unfair to the person who produced the work, who doesn't have a chance to learn from or correct his or her mistakes • Places an additional burden on the rest of the team
Project manager decides: Project manager reviews all work to see if it meets acceptability criteria; contacts anyone who produces unacceptable work; and gives that person suggestions for improvement and a 48-hour deadline to revise.	• Gives the person a chance to correct mistakes • Enables quick notification that the work was unacceptable	• Places the entire burden on the project manager
Team decides: All team members review the work and e-mail the project manager, who then communicates the concerns (without mentioning names) to the person with a 24-hour deadline to revise.	• Avoids burdening the project manager with sole responsibility for deciding whether something is acceptable • Makes the feedback anonymous (the person does not know who found the work unacceptable)	• May take longer to notify the person of the team's concerns

TABLE 3.2. Methods for responding to a member who has produced unacceptable work

hypothetical missed deadlines is much less stressful and time-consuming than panicking at the last minute over how to proceed when one or more teammates have not done their work.

Figure 3.2 illustrates a team charter. Note that the tone is informal and that the charter makes good use of formatting (including boldface headings and bulleted and numbered lists) to make information easy to find. The team charter should be stored in a central place (and/or e-mailed to the entire team) so that team members can use it for reference.

Team Charter

Broad Team Goals

1. Clearly communicate the "bottom line" meaning of our results throughout the report.
2. Impress the instructor with the amount of effort we have put into collecting and analyzing our data.

Measurable Team Goals

1. Meet all six of the evaluation criteria listed on the assignment sheet.
2. Meet or beat all deadlines.
3. Obtain data from at least 15 users.
4. Follow all eight guidelines for tables and figures listed in the instructor's PowerPoint presentation.

Personal Goals

- Aaron: Improve management and teamwork skills.
- Bryan: Improve writing skills (be less wordy).
- Yolan: Improve writing skills (improve organization and grammar).
- Mandy: Improve technology skills (especially PowerPoint) and teamwork skills.

Individual Commitment

- Aaron, Yolan, and Mandy are all willing to put in 100 percent effort.
- Bryan would like to put in 100 percent effort but doesn't know whether his job will allow him to commit that much time. He is willing to accept a slightly lower grade if it turns out he cannot keep up.

Other Concerns

- Yolan is worried that her grammar skills may need a lot of work.
- Mandy has done only one PowerPoint presentation before but really wants to improve her tech skills and will work hard to learn.
- Aaron is usually unable to check his e-mail in the evenings and during weekends but will try to check at least twice every school day.
- Bryan is just worried about his job interfering.

Conflict Resolution

If we experience conflict that is not resolved after 30 minutes of respectful discussion of the points, we will present both sides to the instructor and ask him to decide.

Missed Deadlines

If a team member misses a deadline, the project manager will send a "gentle reminder" e-mail. If that team member does not respond within 24 hours, the project manager will contact the instructor, describing the problem. If there is some extenuating circumstance (e.g., personal emergency), the project manager will contact the rest of the team for input on how to proceed.

Unacceptable Work

If a team member turns in work that is clearly unacceptable (e.g., leaves out important information; has major errors; does not meet the assignment criteria; clearly does not meet the team goals of emphasizing the bottom line throughout), other team members should report their concerns to the project manager. The project manager will then contact that team member with a list of concerns and suggest a deadline (usually 48 hours) for when a revised copy of the work is due. If that team member is confused about why the work is unacceptable, that person should seek assistance and e-mail the project manager explaining his or her progress. We want to note that there is no shame in seeking outside assistance!

FIGURE 3.2. Team Charter

Exercises

1. Return to the scenario of Kelly and Sean's group at the beginning of this chapter. How might a team charter have helped team members through some of the difficulties they experienced?

2. Have you ever been on a team with a negative contributor? What made this person a negative contributor? How could he or she have avoided this? What are some ways other than failing to follow through on commitments that can make someone a negative contributor?

3. Have you ever been on a team in which different people had different ideas about what the project should be, do, or look like? At what point in the project did you recognize these different perspectives? How might a team charter have helped your group handle these different perspectives?

The videos in this textbook are directly based on the interactions of actual student teams. Before you complete any of the video exercises, take a moment to watch the introductory video on the Team Writing *Web site, which describes how the videos were produced and created.*

4. View Team Video 5: Jayme, Megan, and Joe on the *Team Writing* Web site. List three problems this group seems to be having and explain how a team charter might have addressed these problems.

Team 5

CHAPTER 4

Getting Started with the Task Schedule

The **task schedule**, which has been mentioned several times in previous chapters, is the most important document a team produces for managing itself. A task schedule keeps the team on track by documenting who does what by when. Moreover, a task schedule helps the team plan the details of the project so that there are no surprises at the end. This chapter takes you through the steps of producing a task schedule that will help your team implement a layered collaboration. This chapter focuses on four steps:

1. Identifying major tasks

2. Assigning tasks to team members

3. Scheduling the tasks in layers, providing multiple opportunities to comment or revise one another's work

4. Balancing the workload

◆ Identifying Major Tasks

The first step in producing a task schedule is to brainstorm the major tasks that the team will have to perform. Resist assigning tasks to individual team members at this point. Instead, concentrate on making sure that all parts of the project are covered. Listing tasks is a brainstorming activity and is appropriate for face-to-face collaboration.

For example, a team working on a **scientific research report** might identify the following tasks:

Project management
Collect data
Write
    Introduction
    Methods

Results
Discussion
Abstract
Initial topic proposal
Works cited

A team working on a **proposal** might identify the following tasks:

Project management
Research
    Identify audience needs and all relevant stakeholders
    Identify problems with status quo and collect documentation
      of problems
    Investigate potential solutions and costs
Write
    Statement of problem and justification for proposal
    Overview of options
    Cost-benefit analysis and breakdown
    Recommendation and rationale
    Cover letter
    Executive summary
Create presentation slides
Rehearse and deliver final presentation

A team creating a **Web site** might identify the following tasks:

Project management
Write initial topic proposal
Research client
    Obtain technical information for site from client
    Find out client's needs and preferences for the site
Design
    Site layout (number of links or sections on home page)
    Home page layout
    Content page layout
    Graphics
Revise content from client for consistency, Web-friendliness
Assemble the site on test server
Test and revise the site
    Create usability script and set up tests
    Run tests with three users for usability, broken links
    Make revision tests
Upload to live site
Write instructions for maintaining the site
Write final report for instructor

As the differences in these three task lists demonstrate, your task list needs to be specific to *your* team's project. Some projects will consist primarily of research and writing; other projects will involve additional components, such as preparing presentations, uploading Web sites, or coordinating with other people and teams. Be sure to read your assignment guidelines carefully, and work together with your team to come up with a complete list of tasks. The more complete your list is now, the less you will have to figure out on the spur of the moment later.

◆ Assigning Roles: Motivation versus Experience

Christopher Avery, a consultant on leadership and teamwork, states that when a team assigns roles, matching motivation is far more important than matching skills: "If members don't have the required skills, a high performance team will improvise. The same is not true for motivation, however. Every team performs to the level of its least invested member" (2001). In other words, it is more important to assign team members to tasks that they are motivated to learn or do than to tasks with which they already have experience.

One of the biggest problems with layered collaboration in educational settings is that team members often divide up tasks by expertise (that is, the most experienced writer does most of the writing; the most experienced technical person does most of the computer work) rather than by what will make for the best learning experience. Although this division certainly makes sense and is efficient, it also limits team members' opportunities to develop skills in their weak spots. Team members need to take responsibility for making their time on the project a productive learning experience. Such "on the job" training mirrors the corporate world, where managers will sometimes assign tasks to particular workers in order to make them better-rounded employees.

Not only does dividing tasks up by motivation rather than experience benefit individual team members, but it may also benefit the team. Often, a motivated novice will perform at least as well as a bored expert, especially if the novice can contact an expert as a resource for specific questions. An expert who is bored with a task will put in less effort and be less receptive to the team's feedback than a novice who is eager to show that he or she is able to do the job.

Teams can avoid having to choose between motivation and experience by assigning members a **primary task** that they are motivated to learn and a **secondary, advisory task** that makes use of their existing expertise. The assignment of a secondary task allows each team member to serve as an adviser or primary "go to" person in case another team member completing a given task has questions or runs into difficulties. This structuring is similar to that of workplace teams, in which experienced employees focus on gaining new, more complex skills while at the same time helping newer employees learn more routine skills.

For example, if someone on your team has done numerous Power-Point presentations or has years of experience writing proposals, this person should serve as an adviser to another team member who is eager to learn this skill. Not only will the novice be able to draw on the expert's advice, but the expert will also have the opportunity to consolidate his or her knowledge on the topic by teaching someone else. Novices often ask interesting questions that challenge more experienced colleagues to reexamine what they think they know and approach the problem from a new perspective. This explains the adage "If you want to truly learn something, then teach it!"

Assigning roles by motivation rather than experience may also help your team avoid a problem that is particularly common in student teams: a **gendered division of labor**, in which women complete writing tasks and men complete technical work. This tendency is at least partly due to a culture that associates tools and equipment with men and language skills with women and is often reinforced on student teams, particularly when team members do not know one another well. Assigning tasks according to what team members want to learn rather than what they already know how to do can help a team break out of traditional, gendered role assignments.

As a team, review the team preparation worksheets that team members completed in Chapter 3, "Getting Started with the Team Charter" (see Figure 3.1), examining what each person perceived as his or her strengths and learning goals for the project. Then discuss how to arrange the project so that motivated teammates can acquire new skills while still having the security of a more experienced adviser who can answer questions or help out if they get "stuck." This information about primary and secondary roles (and any concerns about these roles) should be added to the team charter.

◆ Scheduling the Tasks

Once your team has assigned primary and secondary roles and recorded these in the charter, look over the team preparation worksheets (Figure 3.1) and team charter again to refresh your memory about any scheduling concerns the team needs to keep in mind. Be sure to also review all of the instructor's deadlines in the assignment guidelines.

The project manager should prepare a rough draft of the task schedule, being sure to include plenty of opportunities for team members to revise and comment on one another's work. Although you can find complicated project-management software for maintaining an updated task schedule, a simple table prepared as a word-processing document or a spreadsheet is just as effective for most school projects. Figure 4.1 gives instructions for creating a task schedule in Microsoft Word. You can also download a spreadsheet formatted for a task schedule from the *Team Writing* Web site at <bedfordstmartins.com/teamwriting>.

To create a task schedule table in Microsoft Word, complete the following steps:

1. Go to the **Insert** tab and click on **Table**. Next, click on **Insert Table**.
2. Type 5 for the number of columns and 20 for the number of rows.

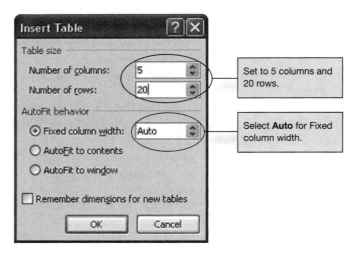

3. Select **Auto** for a fixed column width.
4. Press OK.
5. Enter the words Deadline, Task, Who, Contribution Value, and Status in the first row.
6. Resize the columns:
   a. Hold the cursor over the column boundaries until it changes into the resize pointer ▐▌.
   b. Click the pointer and wait for a faint vertical line to appear.
   c. Drag the pointer until the column is the width you want.
7. To insert new rows, right-click within the table to bring up a menu. Mouse over **Insert**, and then click **Insert Rows Above** or **Insert Rows Below**.

FIGURE 4.1. Instructions for creating a task schedule in Microsoft Word

Once the project manager has created a rough draft of the task schedule, he or she should send it to team members for review before their next meeting. This gives them a chance to reflect on the task schedule and think of ways it might be improved. At the next meeting, the team can work together to revise the schedule to everyone's satisfaction and assign contribution values (discussed in the next section).

◆ Balancing the Workload

One of the biggest problems with collaboration in student teams is the **unequal division of labor**. Unequal division of labor is also present in workplace settings, but typically this is not a problem because it is common for employees to dedicate different amounts of time or effort to a project. In the classroom, however, the assumption usually is that everyone will contribute equally to the project. Thus, student teams have a challenge not often found in workplace teams: distributing the workload so that everybody contributes roughly equally to the project.

To help balance the workload fairly, the team can work together to estimate a contribution value for each task. Contribution values can be measured on a five-point scale (where 5 = difficult, time-consuming task critical to group success and 1 = relatively easy, noncritical task). These contribution values can then be totaled for each team member to get an approximation of how much everyone is contributing to the group. The goal should be for each team member to contribute roughly equivalent amounts (unless one team member has negotiated to receive a lower grade in exchange for less work—see Chapter 3, "Getting Started with the Team Charter").

Figure 4.2 shows one team's task schedule worksheet. Each task is clearly assigned to a team member and has a clear-cut deadline. In addition, each task has a contribution value that the team has agreed on. When the contribution values are totaled, it is clear that all three team members are doing roughly equivalent work but that Amy is doing slightly more than the other two team members. Thus, if additional tasks should come up during the project, Steven and Luke should volunteer for those tasks.

Common Mistakes Students Make When Assigning Contribution Values

Your instructor will probably look over your task schedule and the contribution values your team has assigned in order to make sure that the team is crediting work appropriately. Student teams tend to underestimate the amount of effort required to produce good writing (which often requires substantial revision) and to overestimate the amount of effort associated with technology tasks. Be aware of these tendencies when your team assigns values.

◆ Technology and Tools for Task Schedules

To maintain the task schedule for short projects, teams should probably use familiar and uncomplicated tools such as tables created with a word-processing program or spreadsheets. However, when projects are long and complex, your team may benefit from using more sophisticated scheduling and project-management tools. Following is a brief overview of common tools for keeping track of projects.

TASK SCHEDULE

Amy is the group writing expert. Steven is the group technology expert.

Deadline	Task	Assigned to	Contribution value	Status
9/4	Write topic proposal	Amy	2	
ongoing	Maintain task list and minutes	Amy	3	
9/13	Collect data	Steven	5	
9/14	Enter data and perform initial analysis	Steven	3	
9/20	Write introduction	Luke	3	
9/20	Write methods	Steven	3	
9/20	Write results (with basic graphs)	Luke	5	
9/20	Write discussion	Luke	4	
9/22	Suggest revisions (detailed)	Amy	3	
9/22	Suggest revisions (global issues only)	Steven	2	
9/28	Implement revisions	Luke	5	
ongoing	Help Luke format final graphs in Excel	Steven	1	
10/1	Write abstract for report	Steven	2	
10/1	Make final edits to report	Amy	2	
10/3	Create presentation	Amy	4	
ongoing	Help Amy with presentation	Steven	1	
10/4	Suggest revisions to presentation	Luke	1	
10/4	Suggest revisions to presentation	Steven	1	
10/6	Revise and deliver presentation	Amy	5	

Team member: **Amy**   Total contribution: **19**
Team member: **Steven**   Total contribution: **18**
Team member: **Luke**   Total contribution: **18**

FIGURE 4.2. Task Schedule
The project manager typically prepares the first draft of the task schedule, assigning names and dates to each task. The team then revises the schedule as needed and collaborates to assign contribution values from 1 to 5 for each task. The task schedule offers several opportunities for team members to comment on and revise one another's work. The Status column is for recording when tasks are completed.

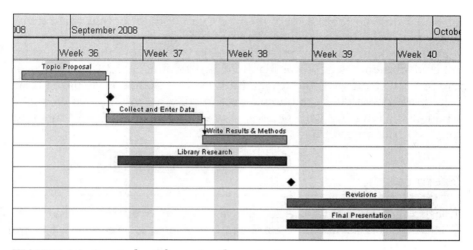

FIGURE 4.3. Gantt chart for a simple project
Black diamonds indicate milestones, and lines with arrows indicate dependencies.

Gantt Charts

A Gantt chart is a type of horizontal bar chart for visualizing the start and end dates of various tasks on a project (see Figure 4.3). Some Gantt charts even show dependencies (when starting one task depends on completing an earlier task). Gantt charts are particularly popular in software development.

One drawback of Gantt charts is that they do not show the complexity of the individual tasks—or the amount of team resources required to complete these tasks—and thus may not provide an accurate representation of the project workload.

Project-Management Software

Many companies purchase project-management software to help supervisors keep track of multiple ongoing projects. These tools often have built-in Gantt charts and other scheduling features as well as tools for adjusting employee workloads and allocating company resources. One of the most popular (and most expensive) options is Microsoft Project. Project-management software is rarely free, but many software companies offer free preview trials. Because most project-management software is built with the upper-management company executive in mind, it may be overkill for your school-based project.

Wikis

A wiki is a collection of Web pages that allows those with access to make changes and add new pages. Teams can place a copy of the task schedule on a private wiki that all team members can update to note when items are completed. Most wikis have a revision-history feature that allows the team to track any changes made. The team can also use the wiki to store other documents, such as assignment instructions and PDFs related to the project. (Note: A Web-based editor such as Google Docs has similar functionality but does not allow teams to store external documents. See Chapter 6, "Revising with Others," for more information on tools that help you collaborate.)

Exercises

1. Take a careful look at the task schedule in Figure 4.2. What common team problems might this task schedule help prevent? Why? What could be done to improve this task schedule?

> *The videos in this textbook are directly based on the interactions of actual student teams. Before you complete any of the video exercises, take a moment to watch the introductory video on the* Team Writing *Web site, which describes how the videos were produced and created.*

2. Review Day One of Team Video 2: Shelly, Will, and Ben on the *Team Writing* Web site. Write up a task schedule that will take the team through drafting and revising 10 survey questions, administering the survey to 30 students, and writing a two-page document describing the survey results. This section of the project should take two weeks from brainstorming to turning in the survey to the instructor. Be sure to build in opportunities for commenting on and revising one another's work.

Team 2

Work Cited

Avery, C., with Walker, M. A., & O'Toole, E. (2001). *Teamwork is an individual skill: Getting your work done when sharing responsibility.* San Francisco: Berrett-Koehler Publishers.

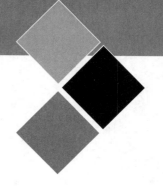

PART 2

Writing Together

CHAPTER 5

Constructive Conflict

Susan, a member of a team working on a Web site for a small business, expresses her frustration with a teammate:

> **Susan:** *I was really upset when Rene just went off and did a draft of the whole Web site. I was really aggravated.*
>
> **Interviewer:** *You said before you had problems with the quality of the site. Is that why you were aggravated?*
>
> **Susan:** *Yeah. Most of the project time was kind of like me biting my tongue to her because I'm not wanting to say anything to her.*
>
> **Interviewer:** *What do you think would have happened if you had said something?*
>
> **Susan:** *Well, she didn't seem like a conflict-like person, so I mean it probably could have been talked out. But I think it would have hurt her feelings, like her site wasn't good enough or something.*
>
> **Interviewer:** *As it is, do you think you hurt her feelings?*
>
> **Susan:** *No. I don't think she knows the rest of us were unhappy.*
>
> **Interviewer:** *Now, several times during the project, Rene said stuff like "This is only a draft" and encouraged you all to make changes to the site or start over from scratch. What did you think when she said things like that?*
>
> **Susan:** *Like "What's the point?" She already did it. It was supposed to be a group thing.*

Susan's comments point to what is the number one problem on some student teams—a lack of substantive conflict. Such teams suffer from a phenomenon called "groupthink," in which creativity and discussion become stifled in favor of a single, group perspective. Such teams suppress any disagreement in the name of group harmony. As a consequence, the team fails to fully consider the merits and drawbacks of competing solutions: the first solution proposed—and not the best solution—dictates how the team proceeds.

In contrast to the conflict avoidance frequently seen on student teams is **constructive conflict**—the healthy, respectful debate of ideas and competing solutions to a problem. Constructive conflict is essential for anticipating problems and working through the pros and cons of different approaches to find the best possible solution. As an operations research manager with more than 20 years of combined military and private-sector experience puts it, "The person who disagrees with you the most is the person whose input you need the most."

The term "constructive conflict" was coined to stress the productive, beneficial role that healthy conflict plays in problem solving. Constructive conflict occurs when two or more people who share the same goal nonetheless hold different ideas about how to accomplish that goal. In carefully debating their different ideas, these people work together to find an optimal solution to a problem.

When team members engage in constructive conflict, they

- **Present evidence and reasons in support of their ideas.** People engaged in constructive conflict do not make emotional arguments or insist that others should listen to them because of their experience or credentials. Constructive conflict involves taking the time to explain the reasoning behind a position.

- **Listen closely to others' viewpoints.** To show that you are a good listener, paraphrase the viewpoint of those you disagree with and ask them to confirm that you have accurately represented their position.

- **Carefully consider the merits and drawbacks of all opinions presented.** Ask the people you disagree with to provide more evidence supporting their position so that you can fully weigh the pros and cons of the issue. Make sure that you have all the information available.

- **Work toward a solution by building and improving on all ideas presented.** Don't just listen to disagreement; try to build on it. Take the time to understand the underlying problems, and use this understanding to think of new alternatives and approaches to the problem.

If your goal is to have the best product possible, you should welcome constructive conflict because it exposes flaws that, when addressed, will lead to an improved product.

One of the biggest differences researchers have found between student and professional teams is that students tend to shut down conflict prematurely. Whereas professionals value conflict and competing ideas as essential to finding the best solution, students often feel that the discussion of competing ideas inhibits group progress. In fact, on a list of problems that student teams experience, business researchers ranked too little conflict and shutting down conflict prematurely as the top problems (Forman & Katsky, 1986). In other words, a major failure of many student teams is reaching a solution too quickly—before the merits and drawbacks of all the options have been fully weighed and considered.

As evidence of the importance professionals place on constructive conflict, consider the results of a survey taken by 49 experienced scientists and engineers at NASA. These professionals, who worked on projects requiring both complex problem solving and technical expertise, rated the factors shown in Table 5.1 as critical to the working of a successful team (Nowaczyk, 1998).

Of the top nine factors identified as critical to team success, more than half concern constructive conflict (items 3, 4, 5, 7, 8). The NASA scientists and engineers in the survey highly valued open, critical, and healthy debate over various solutions to the problem. During such healthy debates, the discussion focuses on the scientific and technical merits of various solutions; team members take the time to explain their ideas to one another; critical evaluation of ideas is encouraged; and team members don't take disagreements over solutions personally but see them as part of the necessary work of the team.

Not surprisingly, in a separate questionnaire, these NASA scientists and engineers identified the failure to respond productively to constructive conflict as the number one problematic team behavior. In particular, they were harsh on colleagues who "believe that their technical status insulates

Factor	Mean Importance Score (1 = no importance; 5 = very important)
1. The team has enough time and resources to complete the task.	4.7
2. There is a sense of "team responsibility" among team members.	4.6
3. The team openly and critically debates various solutions to the problem based on their scientific and technical merits.	4.5
4. The team engages in "healthy" debate over various approaches to the problem or task early on.	4.4
5. During its lifetime, the team experiences a point at which it steps back and critically examines where it is going.	4.4
6. Working on the project is professionally rewarding to individual team members.	4.3
7. Not all team members may agree with the approach or method taken to completing the task but are supportive of the team decision.	4.3
8. Debate and critical evaluation of members' ideas are encouraged.	4.3
9. Team members take the time to explain their ideas and methods so that team members learn from one another.	4.3

TABLE 5.1. Factors NASA professionals rated as important to a successful team

their opinions from evaluation by other team members." This behavior was seen as a problem precisely because it shut down a critical and rational discussion of the merits of various ideas and solutions. Team members who insist on their own ideas without listening to the concerns and criticisms of their teammates become an obstacle to group success—no matter what their knowledge or skill level.

Clearly, these NASA scientists and engineers viewed healthy, critical debate as essential to a successful team. This same spirit of healthy debate is needed whether the team is refining a chemical process, writing a proposal to purchase new hardware, developing an online store, or testing the safety features of a new production plant. This chapter helps you distinguish between the constructive conflict necessary for good teamwork and the destructive conflict that occurs when team members react emotionally to criticism or refuse to reconsider ideas. This chapter also provides suggestions for creating a team infrastructure that will lay the groundwork for constructive conflict.

Although this chapter advocates constructive conflict, you should not therefore assume that *all* conflict is good. Constructive conflict is a productive debate of the merits and drawbacks of ideas in pursuit of the best solution to a problem. However, conflict can become destructive when team members refuse to reconsider their positions, mock or ridicule others, treat questions about their ideas as personal attacks, or use emotional appeals rather than evidence and reason to support their positions. Table 5.2 outlines the differences between constructive and destructive conflict.

Constructive Conflict	Destructive Conflict
Presenting evidence and reasons in support of ideas	Making emotional arguments; insisting that others should listen to you because of your experience or credentials
Accepting questions and criticisms of your ideas as good for the group	Treating questions and criticisms as personal attacks
Listening closely to others' viewpoints	Rejecting others' viewpoints before you fully understand their position
Asking others to present evidence supporting their positions so that you can make a reasoned decision	Mocking or ridiculing others' positions
Building on others' ideas and suggestions	Ignoring or dismissing others' ideas
Disagreeing in order to find the best solution	Disagreeing for the fun of a fight
Being willing to change your mind	Refusing to reconsider your position

TABLE 5.2. Characteristics of constructive versus destructive conflict

◆ Creating a Constructive Infrastructure for Your Team: Five Key Strategies

Unfortunately, goodwill and responsible behavior alone will not necessarily lead to constructive conflict. The following strategies will help lay the groundwork for constructive conflict in your team.

1. Clarify roles and responsibilities up front in a task schedule. Many unproductive conflicts occur because team members are unclear and anxious over what is going to happen next. Team members often have different work styles and expectations for the project; if they don't have a clear understanding of their responsibilities and deadlines, their work styles tend to come into conflict just when the team is under the most pressure to finish. As a consequence, one team member will usually back down and let someone else take over. In other words, the team will have maximum destructive conflict and minimum constructive conflict. Taking time at the beginning of the project to prepare a task schedule will eliminate unneeded tension.

2. Include revision in the task schedule and allow for plenty of time to implement revisions. If team members know from the beginning of the project that another team member will revise, edit, or critique their work, they are less likely to take such criticisms personally because they know that such critique is that person's job. Similarly, if team members know that the schedule includes time for revisions—and that they are *expected* to revise one another's work—they will be less anxious about the direction that work takes.

3. Lay some ground rules for conversation. Following are some typical guidelines for conversation among team members:

- **Set aside time for brainstorming.** During a brainstorming session, no judgments or criticisms of ideas are allowed. The goal is to hear from everyone and generate as many ideas as possible before weighing the costs and benefits of each approach.

- **Get input from everyone in the group.** Before proceeding to any decision making, the project manager or a group facilitator should make sure that everyone has contributed an idea or opinion. This strategy can work very effectively with e-mail: team members privately e-mail their ideas to the project manager, who compiles them anonymously and distributes them with the next meeting agenda.

- **Restate ideas.** This guideline works particularly well when team members do not seem to be listening to one another. The group can establish a rule that after a person has expressed an opinion, another group member has to summarize and restate that opinion *to the satisfaction of the original speaker*. The group does not move on until that person's opinion has been satisfactorily repeated by the group. This strategy slows down heated debates and ensures that each person's opinion is fully heard *and understood* by the group.

- **Set time limits.** Tired people are more likely to go off on tangents or engage in other unproductive behaviors. Set a time limit on conversations and discuss in advance what will happen if the group still has unresolved issues at the end of that time period.

4. Decide in advance how impasses (stalemates) will be handled. Methods for resolving a disagreement when the team seems at an impasse include the following:

- **The group finds consensus.** Discuss the issue until consensus is achieved.

- **The majority rules.** Vote and adopt the majority decision.

- **The supervisor decides.** Take the issue to a supervisor, subject-matter expert, instructor, or other authority for a decision.

- **The client (or target audience) decides.** Ask the client or a member of the document's target audience (that is, a potential user or reader) for an opinion. As one workplace manager said, "This is easy for me. I always just ask the client what they prefer." School projects do not always have a clear client or target audience—or it may not be practical to contact that audience for input. In such cases, you might ask one or more classmates to serve as your target audience and to offer their opinions.

5. Establish team priorities in a team charter or a project plan. This is a particularly useful strategy for large projects. For instance, team members can decide which audience for a document is their priority or whether conciseness is more important than including all of the details. When disagreements occur, they can refer back to the charter to help them weigh the various options.

See also Chapter 6, "Revising with Others," for more specific advice on how to have constructive discussions about revision on your team project.

Exercises

1. Reread the interview with Susan at the beginning of this chapter. Which of the five key strategies listed in the section "Creating a Constructive Infrastructure for Your Team" do you think would have been *most* helpful to this team? Why?

2. Have you ever been on a team—in school or in some other setting—whose members either avoided conflict to the group's detriment or engaged in destructive conflict? What strategies recommended in this chapter might have improved the team's functioning?

The videos in this textbook are directly based on the interactions of actual student teams. Before you complete any of the video exercises, take a moment to watch the introductory video on the Team Writing *Web site, which describes how the videos were produced and created.*

---

3. View Team Video 4: David, Veronica, and Adam on the *Team Writing* Web site. Answer the following questions about this video:

Team 4

a. What model of collaboration does this team seem to be using? (See Chapter 1, "Planning Your Collaboration.")

b. Review Table 5.2, "Characteristics of Constructive versus Destructive Conflict." Which characteristics of constructive or destructive conflict does this team seem to be demonstrating? Provide specific examples.

c. What specific behavioral changes did David make between Part I and Part II of the video that improved team collaboration? List as many specific changes in David's speech, body language, attitude, and verbal interactions as possible.

d. What if David's behavior had not changed so dramatically? Which one or two of the five strategies for creating a constructive infrastructure do you think would be *most* helpful for this team in Part I of the video?

4. Once you have completed question 3, read Appendix F, "Responses and Outcomes for Team Video 4." Considering the outcomes of this project and reactions to the team, what do you think are the major lessons to be learned from this team? Refer to specific concepts from the chapter.

5. View Team Video 5: Jayme, Megan, and Joe on the *Team Writing* Web site. Answer the following questions about this video:

Team 5

a. What model of collaboration does this team seem to be using? (See Chapter 1, "Planning Your Collaboration.")

b. Review Table 5.2, "Characteristics of Constructive versus Destructive Conflict." Which characteristics of constructive or destructive conflict does this team seem to be demonstrating? Provide specific examples.

c. Which one or two of the five strategies for creating a constructive infrastructure do you think would be *most* helpful for this team? Why?

6. Once you have submitted your responses to question 5, turn to Appendix G, "Responses and Outcomes for Team Video 5," and read what professional managers said about this team. Now that you have more information, how would your response to question 4c change?

7. Most people viewing this video immediately identify problems with Joe's behaviors. Do you think that Jayme chose effective strategies for "handling" Joe? What would you have done if you were on a team with Joe?

Works Cited

Forman, J., & Katsky, P. (1986). The group report: A problem in small group or writing processes? *Journal of Business Communication, 23*(4), 23–35.

Nowaczyk, R. H. (1998). *Perceptions of engineers regarding successful engineering team design* (No. NASA/CF-1998-206917 ICASE Report No. 98-9). Hampton, VA: Institute for Computer Applications in Science and Engineering.

CHAPTER 6

Revising with Others

In his final interview, Thomas describes his views on suggesting improvements to his teammates' writing:

> **Thomas:** *Unless it's really bad, I don't think it's really my place to tell other people what to do. I mean, they're smart people. If it's good enough, I'm not going to criticize it.*

Eduardo likewise describes a "hands-off" attitude toward other teammates' writing:

> **Eduardo:** *I thought she should have worded that section less strongly. It's not how I would have put it. But she's the one in charge of writing that information, so she can write whatever she wants.*

Lily explains how such a "hands-off" attitude eventually caused resentment on her team:

> **Lily:** *I remember being so frustrated when Elsa did the whole thing. And she didn't get it. She was like "Well, it's just a rough draft if you want to edit it." And I was like "What's the point? You already did it."*

Thomas's, Eduardo's, and Lily's comments illustrate how uncomfortable students can feel when suggesting changes to a teammate's work. Sometimes, the reluctance is due to feelings of ownership—that the person who wrote a section has the right to phrase and organize things the way he or she wants. Sometimes, as Lily suggests, revision seems pointless if the group can simply agree to move forward with what has already been done. At other times, students hesitate to suggest revisions because they fear hurting a teammate's feelings through criticism, or they worry about seeming egotistical, as if they are better than their teammates.

These concerns about revising or critiquing others' work are understandable, but a well-functioning team should be able to overcome this reluctance. Generating a first-rate project involves recognizing that the team owns the work it produces and that every member shares a responsibility to make every part of the project the best it can be. Learning how to revise and critique your teammates' work is an important part of this process—as is learning how to take and use the feedback your teammates provide on your own work.

This chapter presents some strategies for building a strong **revision process** into your team's culture. When team members feel comfortable critiquing and revising one another's work, the team will draw on everyone's strengths and insights and will produce a superior product. Developing a strong revision process and a team culture in which constructive critique is welcomed and encouraged will allow your team to focus on what is best for the project without worrying about hurt feelings or who "owns" a particular section of the project.

◆ Developing a Culture in Which Constructive Feedback Is Encouraged

The quotes that began this chapter were from students who took part in teams whose culture did not promote critique of others' work—and in all three cases, their projects suffered from the lack of feedback and input. These students did not have a team environment that encouraged constructive conflict (see Chapter 5, "Constructive Conflict").

Here are four steps your team can follow to develop a culture in which constructive feedback is encouraged:

- **Build revision and feedback into the task schedule.** Creating a task schedule in which team members are given "credit" for commenting on or revising one another's work not only encourages team members to *give* feedback but also helps them *accept* feedback as part of the necessary work that goes into a successful collaborative document. If writers know that other team members are *required* to provide suggestions for change (or are required to make revisions), they will not take these suggestions or revisions personally. Thus, scheduling revision and feedback into the task schedule creates a team culture in which constructive feedback is simply part of what it takes to get the project done and is not a negative reflection on anybody's work.

- **Decide on a revision process and follow it.** This chapter describes two basic models for revision: feedback and direct revision. Many teams use a combination of these two methods. For instance, a team might use feedback at the beginning of a project to provide global suggestions for a writer and then switch to direct revision at the end. After considering the advantages and disadvantages of these methods (see Table 6.1 on p. 63), your team should decide how revision will be handled at various stages of the project and create a task schedule that reflects this decision.

- **Use writing software that keeps a history of revisions.** This chapter describes three software tools that help with collaborative authoring by tracking all the changes made to a document (see the section "Technology for Collaborative Revising"). These tools allow one team member to revise another member's work while still preserving the original copy. They also make it easy to undo revisions that the team disagrees with and to offer provisional changes that can easily be reversed. The team can use the software to compare different versions of a document and to discuss the pros and cons of individual changes.

- **Include a statement about the importance of revision and feedback in the team charter.** Once your team decides on a revision process, you can note this in the team charter along with a statement acknowledging that the team agrees that providing honest and constructive feedback is essential to a quality project and that all team members agree to provide thorough feedback on one another's work to the best of their abilities.

◆ Two Types of Revision: Feedback and Direct Revision

Teams can handle revisions in two different ways. In the **feedback** method, one team member drafts some text, submits it to others for feedback, and then implements revisions based on this feedback. This method is sometimes referred to as single-author revision because one person maintains primary responsibility for a section of text. In the **direct-revision** method, one team member drafts some text, and another member implements the revisions, directly changing and revising the text of the previous author. This method is sometimes referred to as multiple-author revision because several people share responsibility for shaping the text.

The Feedback Method

The main benefit of the feedback method is that it is easy to implement. Since one person maintains responsibility for a section of text, there are no opportunities for **version-control problems**, in which two people are simultaneously working from different copies of the text and end up writing over each other's changes. Moreover, the feedback method allows the author to compile comments from several people with different perspectives and can also free up other team members to work on other parts of the project because it usually takes them less time to make comments than to implement direct revisions.

The main drawback of the feedback method is that the quality of the text rests disproportionately on the skills, ability, and efforts of one person. If that person is not a good writer, is defensive about receiving feedback, or does not put sufficient effort or time into drafting and revising, the entire product suffers. For this reason, it is very important to select an author who is highly motivated to improve his or her writing and is therefore eager and willing to listen to others' constructive comments. (Remember: motivation is often more important than experience when selecting people for tasks. See Chapter 4, "Getting Started with the Task Schedule," for more advice on assigning team members to tasks.)

Another drawback of the feedback method is the risk of stylistic inconsistency if the team assigns different sections of text to different authors. Even though these authors may be receiving feedback from one another, the document as a whole can sound disjointed and awkward, especially if the authors have different writing styles or "voices." The following instructor comment on one team's draft illustrates the potential drawbacks of the feedback method:

> Much of the background section is written in the first person plural ("we") while everything else is written in the third person. The "solutions" and "recommendations" sections sound as if they were written for a much more technical audience than the rest of the proposal. Overall, the document sounds like you divided each section up without consulting each other much.

Each section of this document relied on the writing skills of a different team member, and the document lacked a unified "voice" and structure. To avoid this problem, many teams that rely on feedback for revising individual sections of text in the early stages of the project may switch to direct revision toward the end of the project, with one person editing the entire document to make it sound unified and coherent.

The Direct-Revision Method

The main benefit of direct revision is that responsibility for the text is shared by several people who can draw on one another's strengths as they directly change, reorganize, and add to the text. Thus, if one person has strong content knowledge about the topic and another has strong writing and editing skills, the team benefits from combining both of these strengths.

The major drawback of direct revision is that the team can end up with two or more different versions of the same document (known as a version-control problem), a situation that can be frustrating and time-consuming to resolve. Version-control problems can crop up when one team member begins revising a document without knowing that another author is also making revisions to the same text. Moreover, in the direct-revision method, meeting deadlines takes on added importance because the original writer cannot make further changes to the text after handing it off without introducing version-control issues. Some of these problems can be alleviated with a Web-based editor such as Google Docs or a wiki. Nonetheless, "handing off" the text from one writer to the next remains a tricky issue in direct revision.

Choosing a Method

Fortunately, you do not have to choose just one of these methods; teams can and frequently do combine them at different stages of the project. For example, a team may rely on the feedback method for global comments on initial drafts and then switch to direct revision to implement minor changes to the wording and formatting as the document nears completion. Or the team can use the two methods simultaneously: a teammate can hand off a document to another writer for direct revision and at the same time ask the other teammates to provide global feedback. Thus, the person implementing the feedback will be different from the person who wrote the initial draft.

Table 6.1 provides a summary of the benefits and drawbacks of feedback and direct revision.

Method	Description	Benefits	Drawbacks
Feedback	One person drafts the text, submits it to others for comments, and makes revisions based on these comments.	• Easy to implement: the team does not have to worry about version-control problems. • Particularly useful for obtaining global comments from several people.	• The team "puts all of its eggs in one basket" by depending on a single writer. • Sections of the text written by different authors can sound different. • Writers can ignore or reject feedback from other group members without discussing it.
Direct revision	One person drafts the text and then hands it off to another team member, who makes revisions directly to the text and then hands it back.	• Draws on the combined strengths of two or more writers. • Particularly useful for making final edits as the document nears completion.	• Easy for one writer to work from the wrong version of the document. • Missed deadlines take on added importance because of the complexity of handing off the text from one author to the next. • Writers can become upset when other authors change their work.

TABLE 6.1. Feedback versus direct revision

The following questions—while certainly not a complete list of the issues your team should consider—can help you select the method or combination of methods that might be best for your team.

Does your team have . . .	**Then use . . .**
A writer who really wants to improve his or her writing skills?	Feedback so that this writer can have the benefit of receiving and implementing suggestions for improving his or her writing.
A member with both content knowledge and strong writing skills?	Feedback since this writer will be in a good position to see the document as a whole and implement large changes across several sections based on feedback.
One team member with content knowledge and another with strong writing skills?	Direct revision followed by feedback: the content expert can draft the document, and the writing expert can directly revise it. This direct revision should be followed up with an additional round of feedback from the content expert to ensure that the writer has not accidentally changed the meaning or introduced mistakes into the text.
A writer who has trouble accepting feedback?	Direct revision since it may be easier for this person to accept changes once they have already been made than to implement changes suggested through feedback.

Whether you use feedback or direct revision, you and your teammates should be willing to suggest (or directly implement) both major and minor changes to one another's writing. Moreover, both methods require team members to be open to *receiving* feedback and seeing changes made to their writing. With the feedback method, writers must be willing to implement as many of their teammates' suggestions as possible. With direct revision, writers must be open-minded when someone else changes their text and avoid becoming committed to a particular way of phrasing or organizing the text. To help you handle feedback productively while using either method, the sections that follow offer tips for making and listening to feedback on writing. (See also Chapter 8, "Troubleshooting Team Problems," for additional advice on how to handle problems with giving or receiving feedback.)

◆ Before You Start: Ground Rules for Revision

When writers submit work to teammates for direct revision or comments, they should take a moment to clarify the state of the draft and what they see as the goals for revision.

- **Clarify the state of the draft.** Does the writer see the draft as nearly final, needing only minor editing and polishing? Or as very rough, needing major reorganization and content changes? Has the writer submitted a draft missing major sections, with plans to add those sections later? Whenever writers hand off a draft to others for comment or revision, they should provide a brief statement summarizing the state of the draft and outlining the types of changes they believe the draft needs. This will help teammates gauge their feedback. For instance, if a teammate believes that a draft needs major changes but the writer sees it as close to finished, that teammate should expect some resistance from the writer and therefore should provide detailed justification for the proposed changes.

- **Clarify the goals of the revision or feedback.** If the project is nearing the final deadline, major suggestions or revisions may be inappropriate. If the draft is very rough, sentence-level editing would be a waste of time because entire sections may be deleted or entirely changed during the revision process. Taking a moment to agree up front on the goals of the feedback can help the team use its time more effectively.

Figure 6.1 illustrates how a writer might ask for feedback from teammates, while clarifying what level of feedback she is looking for. In Figure 6.2, one of the writer's teammates requests direct revision on a draft that is nearly at its final stage.

For their part, reviewers and coauthors need to make sure that they understand the goals of the project as a whole before they respond to the writer. Thus, *before responding to or revising a draft, teammates should take time to review the assignment instructions* to ascertain what the final product should look like.

◆ Providing Effective Feedback and Making Good Revisions

If you have been assigned to provide written feedback to a teammate or directly revise a draft a teammate has prepared, you should take time to provide thoughtful suggestions. You don't have to be certain about every suggestion you propose. After all, other people will be commenting as well, and the team can decide which suggestions are good ones. However,

> TO: Stephen, Tim
> FR: Charlotte
> Subject: Feedback
>
> Hey guys!
>
> I'm attaching a rough draft of the results and discussion sections. These are very rough, and right now the discussion section is just a list of topics to cover. I plan to flesh it out in the next draft. In the meantime, could you give me some comments on the results section? Does the organization/order seem right? Do the charts work? Let me know if you find any errors on them (I spent a long time on these!).
>
> As for the discussion section, could you let me know if I left out any topics that I should be sure to cover in the next draft?
>
> We agreed in the task schedule that you'd have these comments to me by Wednesday morning. I've blocked out some time in my schedule Wednesday night to work on this.
>
> Thanks!
> Charlotte

FIGURE 6.1. E-mail requesting feedback
Charlotte explains the state of both sections of her draft and the different levels of feedback she would like on each section.

> TO: Charlotte
> FR: Stephen
> Subject: Moving toward the final draft
>
> Charlotte:
>
> I've attached the transmittal letter, abstract, introduction, and works cited. I think these are ready to go, but if you see something major, IM me right away. Could you be sure to look over the works cited and make sure I did it right? APA always makes me nervous. Also you might double-check to make sure I got the letter format just the way Professor Powell wants it. I think I did, but it won't hurt to double-check. As for the rest, I think you can just look these over for typos/polishing and making sure they are consistent with the rest of the report.
>
> Thanks!
> Stephen

FIGURE 6.2. E-mail handing off a draft to be directly revised
Stephen clarifies that he considers the document close to final, but he directs his teammate to a few places where she might want to double-check the format.

you should be constructively critical of the draft. This constructive criticism is key to creating a strong final project and is a major part of teamwork (see Chapter 5, "Constructive Conflict").

Before you provide feedback or make revisions on a draft, make sure you completely understand the project's requirements:

- **Review the assignment instruction sheet.** Make a checklist of the criteria for the assignment. Then read the draft and compare it against this checklist.

- **Check against the grading rubric.** If the instructor has distributed a grading rubric (a sheet that lists the evaluation criteria for the assignment), carefully check your team's document against this rubric to make sure that all the criteria are met.

- **Review the team charter.** Make sure you understand the main goals that the team has set forth in the charter.

Because writers often find it difficult to see shortcomings in their own writing, it is important that someone *other than the original writer(s)* check the assignment for completeness and accuracy. The document will always benefit from having a "fresh set of eyes" take a look at it.

Once you understand the project requirements and have reviewed the draft, you are ready to give feedback or implement revisions. Depending on how far along the project is, you can use one of the following checklists to guide your feedback or direct revisions.

 CHECKLIST
Giving Feedback during the Initial, Rough Stage

Begin with praise. In your e-mail to the writer, note one or two things that this draft does really well—even if all you can say is that the draft does a good job getting some ideas on the table.

Identify/fix oversights. Look for parts of the text that do not meet the assignment requirements or do not match what the group decided on.

Suggest/add new material. What else could be included that would strengthen this draft?

Note/revise misleading or inaccurate information. Look for places where the information included is presented in a misleading way or is simply wrong.

Suggest/implement alternative organizations. Do you think the organization could be improved? Would you recommend reordering some of the sections? Or creating new headings to make the material easier to skim? Should the recommendations be in a bulleted list rather than in paragraph form? Should any tables be reorganized to better communicate the data's message?

Identify/resolve inconsistencies in content and argument. Look for inconsistencies in the information and arguments included. You can address inconsistencies in formatting or vocabulary in later drafts.

CHECKLIST
Giving Feedback during the Final, Polished Stage

Begin with praise. Note one or two things in this draft that are improvements over the previous draft.

Identify/fix oversights. Look for parts of the text that do not meet the assignment requirements or do not match what the group decided on.

Note/revise misleading or inaccurate information. Look for places where the information included is presented in a misleading way or is simply wrong.

Identify/resolve inconsistencies in content, organization, vocabulary, and formatting. Look for inconsistencies not only in the arguments and information included but also in the organization, vocabulary, and format. Does the heading style change from one part of the document to another? Does the document use inconsistent terminology for the same thing? Does the font or formatting suddenly change?

Suggest/implement alternative formatting. Do you think a different type of graph or table style should be used? Would you recommend a different heading style or different font throughout?

Correct grammar and style. Fix grammatical errors, wordy sentences, or awkward phrases.

◆ Listening to Feedback and Negotiating Revision

Responding to feedback may be one of the most difficult parts of working on a team. When your teammates offer feedback or revisions, do not respond defensively. If someone notes a problem, assume that there *is* some sort of problem — even if that person has mislabeled the problem or presented an incorrect solution. Do not reject any feedback until you have considered it from all angles.

The ability to receive and accept feedback represents a high level of professionalism that, as a student, you may not have had the opportunity to develop yet. If you have difficulty accepting feedback or criticism from others, the strategies in the checklist on page 69 may be helpful.

Sometimes, you will receive feedback that you agree with but don't know how to implement. At other times, you will receive feedback that is confusing or that you don't understand. In these cases, don't simply ignore the feedback. Ignoring your teammates' feedback can make them feel that you don't value their work and input — or it can make them wonder whether you are lazy or closed-minded.

CHECKLIST
Accepting Feedback

Count to 10. Before responding to feedback, give yourself a chance to recover from your initial reaction.

Ask the person why he or she made this suggestion. You may find that you and the other person agree more than you originally thought.

Understand criticism. Before accepting or rejecting feedback, repeat back the criticism, the rationale, and the proposed solution (if one was supplied), and then ask the person to confirm that you understood him or her correctly.

Receive comments by e-mail. If you have trouble accepting feedback in face-to-face situations, ask group members to send you an e-mail with their comments and suggestions. This gives you a chance to react to these suggestions in private and gives you time to tone down your initial reactions.

Instead of ignoring feedback that confuses you, ask for clarification—or for suggestions about how to implement it. Figure 6.3 illustrates an e-mail from a teammate asking for clarification.

You might also talk to your instructor or a tutor at your university's writing center about how to incorporate confusing feedback. In many cases, your teammates may have correctly identified a problem in your writing but incorrectly identified the solution. A more experienced writer

---

TO: Stephen
FR: Charlotte
CC: Tim
Subject: Stephen's feedback

Stephen:

Thanks for your feedback. There were some really good suggestions, and I've implemented almost all of them. But one comment that you made has me stumped. You wrote, "This figure is really hard to read. There is too much information here." I agree that the figure is hard to read, but I'm not sure how to fix it since all the information seems necessary. Do you have any advice on what to cut? Or a better way to organize it? Tim, do you have any ideas or suggestions? (We're talking about Figure 4.)

Thanks!
Charlotte

FIGURE 6.3. E-mail asking a teammate to clarify a suggestion

might be able to help you step back and troubleshoot the document from a different perspective.

Sometimes, you will receive feedback that you simply disagree with. If this occurs, try to give yourself 24 hours to cool off and then reconsider the feedback with an open mind. Suggestions that seem impossible at first glance often look much more manageable when you return to them later. Also, if you reread the feedback, you may find that you had initially misunderstood or overreacted to what your teammate was suggesting. A 24-hour cooling-off period allows you to respond to feedback more generously.

If, after cooling off, you still disagree with the feedback or revisions, ask other team members to comment on the issue. You could ask the project manager to put the issue on the agenda for the next team meeting—or the project manager could e-mail the team and ask everyone to comment on the section of text under debate. Sometimes, another team member can provide a suggestion or insight that helps you find a new way to revise that incorporates the best of both your and your teammates' viewpoints. If the disagreement continues, make sure that you abide by the conflict-resolution method you decided on in the team charter—and feel good that your team actually had a substantive discussion about an issue. Most student teams suffer from an avoidance of any kind of substantive disagreement (see Chapter 5, "Constructive Conflict").

If you end up rejecting or disagreeing with the feedback or revisions others have offered, you should provide specific reasons that support your point of view. The best reasons are those that are firmly rooted in the instructor's guidelines, the goals agreed on in the team charter, or the reader's needs. Thus, if you are arguing for or against including particular information or adopting a particular organization—and your instructor has not provided you with clear guidelines on the issue—you will have more success supporting your position if you can make the case that this will meet your audience's needs.

In general, you should try to implement every suggestion your peers provide unless you can clearly articulate a good reason not to. See Chapter 8, "Troubleshooting Team Problems," for more advice on how to handle specific problems that can occur when you are revising with others.

◆ Technology for Collaborative Revising

There are many revision tools available that can help simplify collaborative revising. Some tools are particularly useful for keeping track of direct revisions and reversing controversial changes. Others are particularly useful for providing feedback on text. Some tools help reduce version-control problems by keeping a single, centralized copy of the text on a Web server where it can be edited by everyone. This section discusses some of these tools, starting with the simplest.

E-mail Message

The simplest technology for providing written feedback is to type your constructive criticisms and suggestions for change in an e-mail message. This method is best for providing large, global suggestions for revision. It is not as effective for making minor suggestions to specific sections of text since you cannot easily anchor your comments to a particular paragraph, sentence, or word.

Commenting Features

Many word-processing programs have a commenting feature that allows you to make comments in the "margin" of a document. Figure 6.4 shows Microsoft Word's commenting feature. To make a comment, highlight the section of text you wish to comment on, go up to the Insert toolbar, and select Comment. A box in which you can type your comments will appear in the margin of the text. Once you have commented on the document, you can e-mail it to your teammates. (Hint: If your teammates

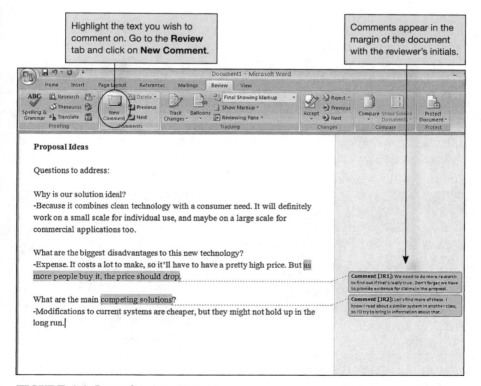

FIGURE 6.4. Inserting comments
Microsoft Word's commenting feature, which allows you to attach comments to specific sections of text, is a good tool for offering detailed written feedback.

use a different word-processing program, you can convert the document to Rich Text Format [.rtf] before sending it. RTF is a universal word-processing format.)

Commenting tools are sometimes combined with Track Changes (see the next section). In this situation, reviewers make large suggestions in the comments and use Track Changes to suggest minor edits and rewordings.

Sometimes, though, when teams use commenting tools, they can end up duplicating their efforts: if several team members are commenting simultaneously, they might spend time pointing out the exact same problems. Moreover, it may be challenging for the writer to collect separate feedback from several people, thereby increasing the chances that some comments get overlooked. To avoid this problem, the team can adopt a "serial commenting" method, in which the document is passed around to teammates one at a time. Each teammate can then respond to the feedback of previous reviewers as well as make additional comments; however, the serial method will lengthen the time it takes to obtain feedback from everyone on the team.

Track Changes

Track Changes is a revision-control feature in Microsoft Word (other word-processing programs have similar tools) that tracks all additions, deletions, and formatting changes to a document. To turn Track Changes on, go to the Review tab and select Track Changes (see Figure 6.5). Using Track Changes, you can make revisions to a document and then give it to other team members, who can then "accept" or "reject" the changes. Figure 6.6 shows a document that has been edited using Track Changes. Figure 6.7 illustrates how other authors can use the reviewing toolbar to implement changes and to switch among different views of the document.

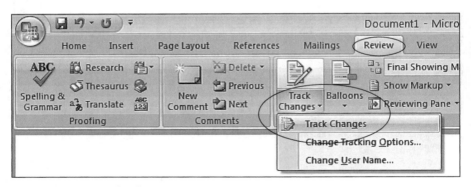

FIGURE 6.5. Track Changes
To turn Track Changes on, go to the Review tab and select Track Changes. Also in the Review tab is a Changes panel that allows readers to accept or reject changes.

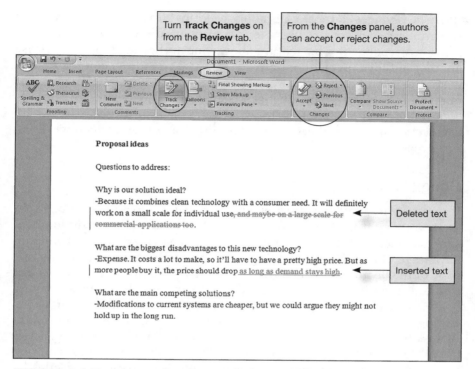

FIGURE 6.6. Document showing tracked changes

Deleted text is indicated by a strikethrough, while inserted text is underlined. Another author can reverse these changes by going to the Changes panel and "rejecting" them.

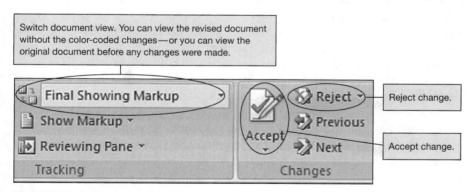

FIGURE 6.7. Review tab

The Tracking and Changes panels allow authors to accept or reject changes made by a previous author and to switch among various views of the document: Final Showing Markup (with Track Changes shown), Final (with Track Changes turned off), and Original (the document before changes were made).

Track Changes is most commonly used for direct revision (although sometimes reviewers also use it to make minor editing suggestions when providing feedback). This feature allows one author to completely revise another author's text without anxiety because coauthors can see exactly what was modified and can easily reverse controversial changes. The main drawback of Track Changes is that coauthors have to carefully coordinate with one another to avoid version-control problems, which can occur when several people are working from different versions of the same text.

Google Docs

If several team members are going to be revising a document extensively, the team may want to consider using a Web-based editing environment such as Google Docs (see Figure 6.8) or a wiki-based editor. The main advantage of a Web-based editing environment is that there is only one copy of the document, which stays on the Web site. Multiple authors can edit and revise it without worrying that someone else has a more recently revised version. However, it is usually best to avoid truly simultaneous editing (when two authors are revising at the exact same time) because there are time lags during which one author might move or delete a section of text that another is working on. Thus, truly simultaneous editing can introduce version-control problems into the process—exactly the problem that a Web-based editing environment is intended to prevent.

Most Web-based editing environments keep a revision history that logs who made what changes when. This revision history can help a teammate identify what was changed recently. Revision histories are also good for undoing revisions by reverting back to an earlier version of the document.

The main drawback of Web-based editors is that they offer far fewer editing features than desktop-based word-processing programs. If your document requires extensive formatting or has lots of tables or figures, you may want to avoid Web-based editors.

Google Docs also allows teams to share and collaboratively edit spreadsheets and presentations. Again, these Web-based tools have far fewer formatting options than the word-processing programs you may be accustomed to.

You can find out more about Google Docs and sign up for a free account for your team at <http://docs.google.com>. See also <www.google.com/google-d-s/tour1.html>.

Wikis

Teams can also use another Web-based editing tool for collaborative revision: a wiki, which is a collection of Web pages that allow users to make changes and add new pages. Wikis are particularly useful for putting together complex sets of information. Whereas a Web-based editor such

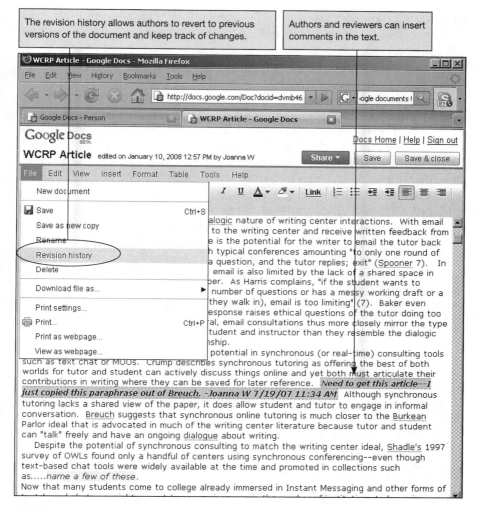

FIGURE 6.8. Google Docs

Google Docs is a free Web-based editor that allows teams to keep a single version of the document online. Using Google Docs, multiple authors can edit and revise the document simultaneously without having to wonder which version is most current. Commenting features can be used to suggest changes, and the revision history feature allows the team to track changes and reject revisions. However, Google Docs has far fewer formatting features than do desktop-based word-processing programs.

as Google Docs essentially focuses on one document at a time, a wiki allows the team to focus on complex relationships among many separate documents. Wikipedia, an online encyclopedia, is a perfect example of a wiki: it consists of a very large network of small documents that are linked together and collaboratively updated. If your team project involves many small, individual documents that need to coordinate together, you may want to consider using a wiki—especially if your team intends these documents to be open to the public to read, comment on, and possibly even revise.

The main advantage of wikis is that they allow the team to store all the documents associated with a project—including task schedules, external reference documents, discussion boards, instructions, and other materials—in one central place. The main disadvantage of wikis is that they have a much higher learning curve than a tool such as Google Docs, which is specifically designed for drafting written documents. When working with a wiki, team members can easily forget where various documents are placed and can miss important information. For this reason, if you use a wiki for your team project, make sure the team discusses up front a standardized method for notifying everyone of exactly *what* has been changed or added and *where* those changes or additions can be found.

It is impossible to discuss all of the wiki options available, but Table 6.2 lists some common wiki features that are particularly useful for collaborative writing.

The following wikis have many of the features listed in Table 6.2:

- Zoho wiki: <http://zoho.com>

- PBWiki: <http://pbwiki.com/education.wiki>

- SocialText: <www.socialtext.com>

In addition, you might want to consult Wikimatrix (<www.wikimatrix .org>), which lists hundreds of current wikis. This site also contains a wizard that helps you select a wiki based on your team's needs.

More Technology for Revision

Depending on the needs of your specific project, you may want to consider some other, less well-known tools for managing collaborative revision, such as Zoho and Gliffy. Zoho, like Google Docs, is a free Web-based editor.* At the time of this writing, it provides a wider range of tools than Google Docs, including an online presentation editor, text chat tools, and project planning tools. It also allows users to import documents directly from Google Docs. However, the sheer number of applications that Zoho supports makes its interface somewhat difficult to navigate. To find out more about Zoho, go to <http://zoho.com>.

Gliffy is online diagramming software that allows you to create flowcharts, diagrams, floor plans, and technical drawings. You can find out more about this tool at <www.gliffy.com>.

---

*In a detailed review in the online magazine *Computer World*, David DeJean compares Zoho, Google Docs, and ThinkFree (another Web-based editor). The article is available at <www .computerworld.com/action/article.do?command=printArticleBasic&articleId=9108799>.

Feature	Description
Free hosting	With free hosting, the wiki exists on someone else's server and requires no setup before using. Most free wikis place a quota on the amount of content your team is allowed to store. Be sure to check this quota and make sure it will be sufficient for your project's needs. Graphics-intensive projects will need large quotas.
WYSIWYG	WYSIWYG (an acronym for "what you see is what you get") refers to software in which the content displayed during editing appears very similar to the final output. Unless your team has some reason for working with the messy details of markup language, you should make sure the wiki has WYSIWYG capabilities.
E-mail notification	Allows you to e-mail your team when changes have been made. A notification method is extremely important.
Export options	If you are required to print your project, you need to pay careful attention to export and print options. Options include exporting to HTML and PDF.
Page history/ revision history	Allows team members to see what was changed and to undo controversial changes if necessary.
Change summary	Allows a team member who revises a page to include a short summary of the changes made.
Revision diffs	Shows the differences between two pages' revisions, making it easy to spot the differences.
Page permissions	Allows teams to make some pages "public" (available to anyone) or "private" (available only to the team). The team can also "lock" some pages so that they are visible but cannot be edited.
Comments/ discussion pages	Provides a system for discussing individual wiki pages. The most common method is a threaded discussion at the bottom of a page.
Attach files	Allows team members to attach external files to their pages. For instance, team members could upload PDFs of articles or other materials related to the project.
Math formulas	Allows math formulas to be displayed in the wiki page. This feature is needed only for technical projects in which writers are expected to provide examples of the calculations or algorithms used during the project.

TABLE 6.2. Wiki features particularly useful for team writing projects

Selecting a Tool

Table 6.3 summarizes the advantages and drawbacks of the various revision and feedback tools discussed in this chapter. Sometimes, your instructor (or supervisor in the workplace) will require you to use certain tools; however, on most projects you will have some choice, so thinking through the pros and cons of various options up front will save you headaches later.

Tool	Advantages	Disadvantages
E-mail message	• Simple to use. • Allows for quick turnaround. • Good for global feedback. Lack of editing features keeps reviewers focused on "big picture" issues.	• Difficult to comment on specific sections, paragraphs, sentences, and words. • Inappropriate for final editing stages.
Microsoft Word commenting tools	• Reviewers can comment on specific sections of text. Comments are off to the side and easily distinguishable from the main text. • Teammates can respond to one another's comments and discuss the pros and cons of various changes. • Can be combined with Track Changes.	• Reviewers may duplicate efforts by making identical comments. • May be difficult to reconcile feedback from different reviewers unless the team uses "serial" commenting, in which each reviewer comments and then hands the document off to the next reviewer for comments.
Microsoft Word Track Changes	• Easy to see what was changed and to switch back and forth between original and revised versions. • Easy to accept or reject changes another author has made. • Can be combined with commenting tools to provide justifications of changes or to query coauthors.	• Only one person can work on the document at a time. • Version-control problems can occur when multiple authors work from different versions of the document, writing over each other's changes.
Google Docs	• Writers are always working from the most current version of the document, so the team does not have to worry about version-control problems. • Combines commenting capabilities with direct revision. • Document resides in a common storage space where the team can keep task schedules and other documents associated with the project.	• Lacks a rich set of formatting tools and is inappropriate for documents that have lots of tables or require extensive formatting features. • Comments are inserted directly into the text, sometimes making the text difficult to read.
Wiki	• Pros are similar to those of Google Docs. • Provides maximum flexibility for creating and linking multiple documents. • The team can make project information public and available for comments or edits from outside audiences.	• High learning curve for many users. • Server may not be stable, and technical support may be unavailable. • May be difficult to export or print documents. • Easy to lose, misplace, or miss key information.

TABLE 6.3. Advantages and disadvantages of revision tools

Exercises

1. Have you ever been on a team in which you noted a problem with a teammate's work but didn't point it out? What stopped you from providing feedback? Now that you have read this chapter, what are some strategies you could use to politely provide suggestions for revision?

2. Review the assignment materials your instructor has provided. Working together with your team, come up with a checklist of items to look for when commenting on or revising one another's work.

3. Pull up a document that your team has already created (or create a new document of "dummy" text), and try editing it with each of the tools mentioned in this chapter. Which tool do you think will be most effective for your team? Why?

4. Do you ever have problems responding positively to feedback or criticism? Which of the strategies outlined in this chapter for responding productively to feedback do you think would be most helpful in improving how you respond to criticism?

5. Review the team charter and task schedule your team has created, and decide which revision tool you plan to use and which revision method (feedback or direct revision) you plan to implement at various stages in the project. Update the task schedule accordingly. Review the sections of the team charter that state overall team goals and methods for handling impasses. Do you think that any of these sections should be updated?

The videos in this textbook are directly based on the interactions of actual student teams. Before you complete any of the video exercises, take a moment to watch the introductory video on the Team Writing *Web site, which describes how the videos were produced and created.*

6. View Team Video 3: Jamaal, Jim, Don, and Tonya on the *Team Writing* Web site. Then turn to Appendix E, "Responses and Outcomes for Team Video 3," and read about this project's outcome. What could this team have done differently to avoid the problems it experienced later? What do you think are the major lessons to learn from this team?

Team 3

CHAPTER 7

Communication Styles and Team Diversity

When they were asked in their final interviews to comment on how individual team members got along, Veronica and David had this to say about each other:

> **Veronica:** *It was a headache because the things that I said weren't being heard. If someone asked a question and I tried to answer it, David especially would interrupt me. . . . So I just started to sit back and not say anything because I got tired of, you know, having to shout to be heard. It felt like it didn't matter what I said; they're not going to listen.*
>
> **David:** *Well, I think Veronica, she might have the worst view of me because she and I just come from different places. With her, I kind of felt like I had to watch what I said because there were some issues there. Do you understand what I'm saying? Whereas with other people, I didn't have to make sure. If I ignored or interrupted them, it wasn't this big issue.*

Veronica and David have conflicting communication styles, among other issues. Whereas Veronica perceives interruptions as a sign of disrespect—an indication that others don't care about what she has to say—David sees interruptions as part of the normal ebb and flow of a debate. He feels that he has to curb his normal style of talking in order to accommodate Veronica and wishes that she could be more like the others in his group. As David notes, he and Veronica "just come from different places." He worries about how she perceives him, and vice versa.

Sooner or later, you will find yourself on a team with someone who "comes from a different place" than you do. This chapter teaches you to take the differences between you and your teammate and turn them into something positive. Key to achieving this positive outcome is understanding the differences in communication styles. Many interpersonal problems occur on teams because team members differ in their assumptions about how they should talk to one another, what constitutes productive behavior, and what constitutes rude behavior. Understanding that people can have different assumptions about what is "normal" communication will help you work with others whose communication preferences differ from yours.

The best teams are those that are easy on people but hard on problems. This chapter teaches you about communication styles so that the merit of an idea or a solution—and not how it was communicated—determines whether or not your team adopts it.

◆ The Benefits of Diverse Teams

A diverse team is one composed of people of different genders, ethnicities, or educational backgrounds or from different geographic regions. Although diverse teams sometimes experience social discomfort as people learn to work together, researchers have found that diverse teams outperform homogeneous ones (teams composed of people with similar backgrounds)—particularly on complex tasks without clear solutions (Cordero et al., 1996). These findings should not be surprising if you think back to Chapter 5, "Constructive Conflict," which showed that teams work best when they experience productive conflict by fully considering the merits and drawbacks of a range of ideas. Teams composed of people from diverse perspectives and backgrounds are likely to propose diverse solutions to problems. Such teams will have more opportunities for such constructive conflict than teams in which everybody thinks and acts alike. Thus, diversity often leads to creativity and innovative problem solving.

Moreover, diverse teams are far less likely than homogeneous ones to propose solutions that work only for a single group of people. For instance, when car air bags first became common in the 1980s, designers and auto manufacturers, who were mostly male, tested them on dummies measuring 5 feet 9 inches—the height of the average American man. Only after many women and children were injured and even killed by inappropriately deploying air bags did automakers realize that this safety device could actually harm people with smaller body frames. Today, air bags are now designed and tested for a range of body types, including pregnant women. If more women had been involved in auto-manufacturing design in the 1980s, this fatal design flaw probably would have been noted and addressed earlier.

However, even if diverse teams didn't have advantages over homogeneous ones, there is at least one practical reason for learning how to work with people different from us: as our culture becomes more global, our workplaces will become increasingly diverse, and therefore homogeneous teams will become less and less common. Learning how to handle diversity successfully is becoming a necessary job skill. Understanding how norms work in interpersonal interactions is the first step in acquiring that skill.

◆ How Differences in Communication Norms Can Cause Interpersonal Conflict

By understanding how norms affect your behavior and your perception of other people's behaviors, you can foster a team environment that reaps the benefits of diversity while minimizing the dissatisfaction that diversity causes. In the realm of communication and other interpersonal issues, a **norm** is a standard of behavior typical of a particular group. An **individual norm** is what a particular member of that group considers to be normal behavior. Norms govern how we think, talk, and act. When team members have conflicting norms, they will have different ideas about what is productive or unproductive as well as conflicting ideas about what is polite, mildly offensive, or just plain rude.

An illustration of different **communication norms** can be seen in how people from different cultures respond to compliments. In the United States, children are usually taught that it is polite to accept compliments, usually by saying "thank you." In Japan and Korea, however, children are taught to deflect or deny compliments by saying "no, no" or "that's not true" (Kim, 2003). A Korean unfamiliar with American cultural norms might think that an American was egotistical for accepting a compliment; conversely, an American might think that a Korean was rude for refusing to accept one. Yet no one way of responding to compliments is inherently better than another—your preference is just a result of what you were brought up to see as normal.

Even within a single culture—especially one as diverse as U.S. culture—there are wide differences in what is considered normal behavior. For instance, some behavior that is considered normal in a crowded area such as New York City may be perceived as rude in other parts of the country. Similarly, what a southerner may view as a polite and necessary conversation-starter might be perceived as an infuriating waste of time by a midwesterner. Even within a particular geographic region, men and women, or people from different social classes, may have different norms. For example, behavior that might be considered normal and appropriate in single-gender settings is often considered inappropriate in mixed company. Similarly, one group of people may find it natural and normal to talk about their accomplishments, whereas another group in the same community may see such talk as egotistical and self-promotional.

Increasing your awareness of social norms can help you reduce unproductive conflict, know how to adjust your behavior to "fit in" to otherwise unfamiliar or uncomfortable social situations, and understand why others might have difficulty fitting in to norms that feel natural to you. This chapter discusses three areas in which different norms often cause conflict in student teams. Before continuing, take the self-assessments in Figures 7.1, 7.2, and 7.3 to see what sort of norms you favor in team interactions. (You can also download a copy of these self-assessments from the *Team Writing* Web site at <bedfordstmartins.com/teamwriting>.)

◆ Understanding Norms

Taking these self-assessments will help you identify what feels like a "normal" discussion, self-presentation, or problem-solving style to you. These self-assessments and the discussion in the rest of the chapter offer three basic lessons:

1. What feels "normal" to you may be different from what feels "normal" to others.

2. People whose norms differ from yours are not necessarily egotistical, insecure, or rude—they may just have different ideas and assumptions about what is appropriate behavior.

3. When working in a group setting, you may need to change your norms—in other words, change your normal patterns of talk or behavior—to do what is best for the group as a whole.

Note

You may find that *none* of the communication and interpersonal styles measured in the self-assessments characterize you—or that you have the characteristics of multiple norms. That's perfectly fine, and far more norms exist than this text could possibly cover. The purpose of this chapter is to expose you to some of the norms *your teammates* may exhibit and to provide you with strategies for interacting with people whose norms you may not share.

Table 7.1 provides information about some common norms and their pros and cons. It provides only a small sampling of the norms that sometimes lead to unproductive conflict in teams. You may find that several of these norms describe you—or that none of them describe you. Or, because most of these norms represent extremes, you may find that you fall somewhere in the middle of the spectrum. The goal here is to recognize that people can have some strong differences in their assumptions about what is appropriate and effective communication and teamwork.

SELF-ASSESSMENT

Each item in the following assessment reflects something that a person might say or think. For each item, indicate how well this statement describes you **when you are interacting with teammates**. Use the following scale:

1 = never (not at all like me)
2 = rarely
3 = sometimes
4 = frequently
5 = always (very much describes me)

Discussion Style

1. When I get a good idea during a team meeting, I say it as soon as possible, even if I have to interrupt to do so.
2. I am careful to wait for my teammates to finish speaking before I jump into a team discussion.
3. My teammates sometimes accuse me of not listening.
4. I nod or agree with teammates while they are talking.
5. I hate feeling as though I have to wait my turn to talk during a team discussion.
6. If I keep getting interrupted during team meetings, I generally give up on trying to talk.
7. I talk over (talk at the same time as) teammates who are trying to speak.
8. I prefer to listen carefully to what my teammates have to say before I form my own opinion.
9. I enjoy challenging my teammates' ideas.
10. If I need to express criticism, I am always careful to avoid hurting my teammates' feelings.
11. When a teammate expresses a new idea, my first instinct is to point out the flaws.
12. When a teammate expresses a new idea, my first instinct is to ask questions.
13. I always say what's on my mind during team meetings.
14. I think it is rude when my teammates never stop to ask me about my opinion.

Add up your responses to the odd-numbered statements. If your score is greater than 25, you exhibit many characteristics of a **competitive discussion style**.

Add up your responses to the even-numbered statements. If your score is greater than 25, you exhibit many characteristics of a **highly considerate discussion style**.

Note: The self-assessments here focus on styles that sometimes come into conflict and are by no means comprehensive. You may find that you score low on both scales or that you exhibit some characteristics of both the competitive and highly considerate discussion styles. In that case, simply choose the description that seems to fit you the best.

FIGURE 7.1. Self-assessment of discussion style

SELF-ASSESSMENT

Each item in the following assessment reflects something that a person might say or think. For each item, indicate how well this statement describes you **when you are interacting with teammates**. Use the following scale:

1 = never (not at all like me)
2 = rarely
3 = sometimes
4 = frequently
5 = always (very much describes me)

Presentation Style

1. I frequently express doubts about my skills, knowledge, or preparation to my teammates.
2. I usually assume that I am one of the least skilled people on a team.
3. I almost never let teammates know that I am having difficulty doing something.
4. I hate it when a teammate who knows less than I do questions my ideas.
5. When I make a mistake, I apologize profusely to teammates, even if the mistake is minor.
6. I often say things to my teammates to show that I don't think too highly of myself.
7. I would rather miss a deadline than admit to a teammate that I don't know how to do something.
8. If I think a project isn't challenging enough for me, I might slack off and let some of my teammates take over.

Add up your responses to statements 1, 2, 5, and 6. If your score is greater than 12, you exhibit characteristics of a **self-deprecating presentation style**.

Add up your responses to statements 3, 4, 7, and 8. If your score is greater than 12, you exhibit characteristics of a **self-promotional presentation style**.

Note: The self-assessments here focus on styles that sometimes come into conflict and are by no means comprehensive. You may find that you score low on both scales or that you exhibit some characteristics of both the self-deprecating and self-promotional presentation styles. In that case, simply choose the description that seems to fit you the best.

FIGURE 7.2. Self-assessment of presentation style

SELF-ASSESSMENT

Each item in the following assessment reflects something that a person might say or think. For each item, indicate how well this statement describes you **when you are interacting with teammates**. Use the following scale:

1 = never (not at all like me)
2 = rarely
3 = sometimes
4 = frequently
5 = always (very much describes me)

Problem-Solving Style

1. I prefer that the team think through an idea completely before we start working on it.
2. I quickly become impatient with long team deliberations.
3. I am always willing to consider new possibilities for solving a problem.
4. When my team is given a technical problem, I prefer that we begin figuring out the technical details as soon as possible.
5. When my team is given a technical problem, I prefer that we make sure we completely understand "the big picture" and end goals before we start thinking about the technical details.
6. I prefer that the team focus on getting things done as quickly as possible.
7. I think it is useful to spend time weighing the pros and cons of different ways to approach a problem before the team begins making any concrete plans.
8. Teams that spend a lot of time talking about ideas up front are just wasting time that could be used actually working on the project.

Add up your responses to the odd-numbered statements. If your score is greater than 13, you exhibit characteristics of a **holistic problem-solving style**.

Add up your responses to the even-numbered statements. If your score is greater than 13, you exhibit characteristics of an **action-oriented problem-solving style**.

Note: The self-assessments here focus on styles that sometimes come into conflict and are by no means comprehensive. You may find that you score low on both scales or that you exhibit some characteristics of both the holistic and action-oriented problem-solving styles. In that case, simply choose the description that seems to fit you the best.

FIGURE 7.3. Self-assessment of problem-solving style

Area	Norm	Definition	Pros and Cons
Discussion style	Competitive	Conversation is a miniature battle over ideas. Speakers tend to be passionate in supporting their ideas, and interruptions are frequent.	Those who hold this norm like the fast-paced conversation and the challenge of publicly defending ideas in the face of competition. However, those who don't share this norm perceive it as rude and disrespectful. Moreover, this norm works against constructive conflict because speakers are more concerned with defending their own ideas than with carefully listening to their teammates. Often, the most aggressive speaker rather than the best idea wins out.
	Highly considerate	Speakers acknowledge and support one another's contributions, and disagreements are often indirect. Interruptions are rare, and the conversation often pauses to allow new people to speak.	Those who hold this norm like the polite tone, concern for others, and equitable conversations that it fosters. However, those who don't share it find these conversations slow-moving and frustrating and sometimes think that highly considerate speakers have nothing important to say. Moreover, this norm sometimes privileges feelings and emotions over constructive criticism of ideas.
Presentation style	Self-promotional	Speakers aggressively display their own confidence and expertise, often criticizing others to make themselves look better.	This norm sometimes benefits people who may expect special treatment for their expertise but is generally harmful to the group dynamics. Self-promotional speakers tend to see asking for help as a weakness and to see criticism as a direct attack on themselves.
	Self-deprecating	Speakers display their modesty and talk about their own shortcomings.	Even though people (especially men) who engage in humorous self-deprecation may be perceived as likable and easy to get along with, this norm can make group members distrust the speaker's ability to do competent work. Sometimes, self-deprecating speakers are perceived as trying to get out of work.

(continued)

TABLE 7.1. Some communication norms and their pros and cons

TABLE 7.1. *(continued)*

Area	Norm	Definition	Pros and Cons
Problem-solving style	Action-oriented	People immediately jump into the details of a problem and start working on a solution right away.	This style is very effective for getting things done quickly, but sometimes groups waste time by working on solutions before they fully understand the problem.
	Holistic	People consider the entire problem as a whole and refrain from proposing solutions until the problem is completely understood.	This style generally helps groups propose better solutions because it ensures that they are solving the correct problem. However, the holistic problem-solving style requires more time. Moreover, action-oriented problem solvers sometimes find this style frustrating to work with.

Being aware of the norms in Table 7.1 can help you avoid thinking negatively about others. For instance, you might realize that competitive speakers are not deliberately being rude but are acting in ways that feel normal to them. Or you might realize that a self-deprecating speaker is not incompetent but is simply being modest. Understanding norms can also help you change your behavior to better fit in to certain social situations. For example, an American businessperson working in Japan, where a considerate conversational style is often the norm, might want to refrain from interrupting others and to avoid any behavior typically associated with a competitive conversational style.

◆ Competitive versus Considerate Conversational Norms

Take a look at the following transcript. It shows the actual discussion of a student team and has not been edited for grammar or completeness. As you read, think about how you would characterize the discussion norms that these speakers seem to hold.

> **Mark:** *Okay. Here [are] my thoughts on organization. This is what I call "pre-applying." Stuff you want to have down before you apply.*
> **Natalie:** *Before you graduate.*

Mark: *Yeah. And then the next section is applying. Then is the interview process, what to do, how to act. And then I thought maybe the last question would be "after the interview."*

Keith: *Okay, I'm not sure I buy into a pre-applying section like that. "Pre" implies a time issue, but these [are] done before you go. "Pre" is incorporating everything except the interview.*

Mark: *Okay, but I'm thinking about the process. . . .*

Keith: *Yeah, but do you think that should be like the way to organize the paper? You see, pre-applying, that seems to incorporate everything to me. Maybe you could say, um, "Curriculum Requirements," "Deadlines." Something like that, you know. . . .*

Mark: *No.*

Keith: *"Pre" is a meaningless title because it would be everything.*

Mark: *No, what . . .*

Natalie: *I think what Mark's saying . . .*

Keith: *I understand, but see, having it all under the title of "pre-applying" doesn't make sense.*

Mark: *When I think about applying, I'm thinking about, July first is when I turn in my materials.*

Keith: *I understand exactly what you're saying, but I don't understand why you need that under that title of "pre-applying."*

Mark: *I think it's a natural process.*

Keith: *I'm suggesting we reword that whole thing.*

Natalie: *Could we say "Things that should be done prior to . . ."?*

Keith: *Find some other way of wording it because the way it's worded right now doesn't make any sense at all.*

Natalie: *Okay, what I'm saying is we could have "Things that should be done prior to the application process" and then "Things that can be done during the process."*

Keith: (talking over Natalie) *We can stress . . .*

Mark: (talking at the same time as Keith) *But when I think "during"* . . .

Mark and Keith both demonstrate a **competitive** conversational style in this exchange. They frequently interrupt each other (and Natalie) and often seem more concerned with making their own points than with listening to what the other has to say. Overall, Keith and Mark both tended to enjoy such exchanges, associating them with a high degree of involvement in the project. Many people find the back-and-forth of competitive conversations exciting and enjoy the challenge of scoring a point or winning others over to their side. In many ways, competitive conversations like this one resemble the types of debates you might see on TV programs such as *The O'Reilly Factor* or *Hardball with Chris Matthews*.

Unfortunately, although competitive conversations allow speakers to battle out ideas, speakers are not really involved in coming to a cooperative solution. For instance, in the preceding conversation, both Keith and Mark advocate for their own ideas without ensuring that they have heard the other's counterposition. Keith states that he understands Mark, but he fails to convince Mark of this. The conversation would have been far more productive if Keith had told Mark "I understand your position to be X" and had given Mark a chance to confirm or deny this understanding. This strategy would have given Mark an opportunity to clarify his reasoning; furthermore, it would have assured him that he could stop arguing for his position and would have allowed him to listen more productively to Keith's criticism.

Even worse, though, is that Natalie is having trouble entering the conversation. One of the problems with competitive conversational styles is that they are **hierarchical**: in other words, speakers who are perceived as having lower status on the team are more likely to be interrupted, ignored, or talked over. On this team, Natalie has consistently been less vocal than her teammates and less assertive when she does speak. As a consequence, her teammates have become accustomed to thinking of her as someone who does not have much to contribute—as someone with less influence than her teammates. Thus, even when she does speak, her teammates have a hard time hearing her: they talk over her and barely consider the suggestion she has made.

Natalie, of course, could be more assertive and speak more competitively, like her teammates. However, this tactic may be difficult for her: as someone out of place in competitive conversations, Natalie has probably been socialized to think of behaviors such as interrupting and talking over others as rude. Unless she has an exceptionally strong investment in the project, Natalie may prefer to stop participating rather than adopt a conversational norm that she finds offensive.

One of the biggest problems with competitive conversations is that they can shut down people who don't share this style and thus can exclude some speakers' ideas. Those who like competitive conversations may think that they are openly debating ideas, but in fact, they are likely hearing and discussing *fewer* ideas than they would if the team had adopted a more cooperative conversational style.

In contrast to competitive conversations, **considerate** conversations are characterized by a high degree of mutual support through questions and what is known as **back-channeling**: providing support through brief statements such as "yeah" and "uh-huh" or by nodding your head. As you read the following conversation excerpt of a team planning a Web site, note what specific strategies the speakers are using to create a considerate conversational environment:

> **Josh:** *What we need to do at this point is figure out what resources we need to have ready so that when we sit down with Front Page, we know what we're going to put in the site.*
> **Rose:** *Oh, okay. Well, we can do that right now.*

Ming: *Yeah.*

Stacy: *Yeah, 'cause like whatever paperwork we need I can pick up this weekend, and then, if you want, we can distribute it out so we can all think of different ways to do it.*

Rose: *Yeah.*

Ming: *You know, I was gonna ask . . .*

Stacy: *I can pick up all the paperwork Friday.* (to Ming) *Sorry.*

Ming: *I was gonna ask if she wanted it like the examples in the online book or like a corporate site. It's 30 pages long.*

Stacy: *I don't think we need to do all 30 pages.*

Ming: *That's what I was askin'.*

Rose: *Just do like a miniature version?*

Stacy: *Yeah.*

Josh: *Yeah.*

Ming: *So do we want it like the online one? Because I wasn't sure about that example.*

Josh: *I thought that's what she wanted.*

Rose: *Should we ask?*

One of the biggest differences between this conversation and the competitive example is that Stacy *repairs her interruption* of Ming halfway through by turning to him and saying "sorry." This simple action gives Ming an opportunity to say what is on his mind. Other effective remarks for inviting silenced speakers to talk include "I'm sorry. What were you trying to say?" or "Ming, you were interrupted just a second ago. Did you have something else to add?"

Moreover, in this conversation, we see speakers *acknowledging ideas* by saying "yeah" and restating ideas rather than immediately tearing them down. We also see team members *asking questions* rather than always arguing for a particular point of view.

A considerate speaking style does not mean that people always have to agree with one another. In the following excerpt, note how Wes and Marissa are able to disagree even while maintaining a considerate communication style:

John: *Well, it sounds like we were going to be addressing our proposal to oil companies, but now we're doing something else?*

Wes: *I was thinking environmental agencies.*

Marissa: *Do you think we could do both? We could do like, we want to propose this to the environmental place so we can go with them to the oil companies? So we can tell them what we want to say to the companies?*

Wes: *Yeah, that could work.* (pause) *But one thing that I was thinking, the proposal would be stronger if it was just one thing.*

Marissa: *I just don't want to lose that focus on the companies themselves.*

> **John:** *So like make oil companies an indirect audience? A secondary audience?*
> **Marissa:** *Yeah.* (to Wes) *You think it's too much to do both?*
> **Wes:** *Yeah, kinda.*

This group eventually ends up agreeing with Wes that the proposal would be stronger with a single, clearly defined audience. What is noteworthy here is that even though Wes and Marissa are disagreeing, they still display a considerate conversational style. Before pointing out problems with Marissa's idea, Wes acknowledges that "that could work." This acknowledgment, as well as John's later restatement of Marissa's idea, most likely helps Marissa accept Wes's criticism that she is proposing "too much." Moreover, Marissa "checks in" with Wes by restating his idea and asking if she has understood correctly. This restatement lets Wes know that he was heard and invites him to elaborate on what he thinks.

Competitive speakers often have difficulty providing positive acknowledgment to their teammates and may even feel that all the agreement and "checking in" in the preceding two conversations sound silly. However, to speakers who have more considerate conversational norms, such agreement is necessary to an effective group, and those who fail to provide it appear self-centered or egotistical.

Competitive speakers can adjust their conversational style, although they may find it frustrating to do so. In fact, Wes (in a later interview) explains how he deliberately curbed some of his competitive instincts:

> **Wes:** *I wanted to say, "No, we can't do both!" That's not going to work. I mean, oil companies aren't gonna adopt solar energy unless they've gone insane! I wanted to say that. But I had to think of how to say it that didn't make her argument sound absurd because I didn't want to do that.*

Later on in the interview, Wes further acknowledged that he was trying to avoid "winning" an argument just based on his conversational style:

> **Wes:** *It's a bad habit I have, but when I want people to do something, I usually try to just keep talking until they finally agree with me. I was trying not to do that here, but it was frustrating. It was slow.*

Wes's efforts to avoid making his teammates defensive seem to have paid off: at the end of this project, everyone on the team (including Wes) reported being highly satisfied with the way the group had worked together. Moreover, although Wes stated several times that he found the debate over their proposal's audience frustrating, his teammates found the discussion useful:

> **Interviewer:** *Do you think this discussion was a productive one?*
> **John:** *Very.*

Interviewer: *Why's that?*

John: *Everybody's just like getting their ideas out and just trying to get a feel for what are we going to do. We figured out what we wanted to talk about in this conversation. So, yeah, it was a very productive day.*

Even though considerate conversation styles generally are good support for constructive conflict, in some cases they can interfere with teamwork if team members feel that they always have to wait for an invitation to speak or are so concerned with preserving people's feelings that they hold back on ideas. The goal is to foster a group style that allows everyone to feel that he or she can contribute while still keeping the team focused on finding an effective solution.

How Can Competitive Speakers Adopt a More Considerate Style?

The following strategies—which are good strategies for any team to follow—help mitigate the silencing effects of competitive conversations:

- **Repeat back or restate ideas before disagreeing with them.**

- **Repair interruptions and other competitive behaviors.** Competitive speakers may find themselves unconsciously interrupting, raising their voices, or speaking over someone. When this happens, they (or anyone else on the team) can repair these actions by turning to the silenced person and saying "I'm sorry. You were saying?" or "David, you were interrupted just a second ago. Did you have something else to add?" or just "Sorry, I didn't mean to interrupt."

- **Check in with quiet speakers.** Every so often, the project manager or other team member should check in with anyone who has not spoken recently by saying "Do you have any thoughts?"

- **Pay attention to body language.** Watch the nonverbal behaviors of your teammates. If any of your teammates start to say something but stop, extend their arm or hand toward the center of the group, or lean far forward in their seat, they may be attempting to enter into the conversation. Whenever your teammates display these types of behaviors, invite them to speak by saying something like "Julie, you look like you have something to say."

- **Engage in uncritical brainstorming.** In uncritical brainstorming, teams set aside a limited period (say 10 minutes) during which no criticisms of ideas are allowed. Team members can build on one another's ideas and ask questions but not point out flaws. The goal of this brainstorming period is to get as many ideas as possible on the table and see what is good about these ideas before finding fault with them.

How Can Considerate Speakers Adjust to Competitive Conversations?

If you are a considerate speaker, you may have to deal with situations in which competitive speech is the norm. Rather than giving up on participating or becoming angry at your teammates, you can use the following strategies for getting your ideas across:

- **Learn how to prevent or forestall interruptions.** To stop a competitive speaker from interrupting, you can use gestures while speaking, such as extending your arm forward or holding up your hand like a stop sign. Such gestures tell others that you are not done yet and have more to say. Simple stock phrases, such as "I'm not finished yet" or "One minute please," can also be good ways to stop interruptions.

- **Speak within the first five minutes of a meeting.** Another non-aggressive strategy for dealing with competitive conversations is to get people accustomed to thinking of you as having something important to say. Louisa Ritter, Telecommunications Chief of Staff for a major investment firm, states, "The longer it goes without you saying something, the longer people are going to ignore you, and by the time you do speak up, people are just going to think you're peripheral to the meeting" (Commonwealthclub, 2003).

- **Find gentle ways to interrupt.** Ultimately, you may need to learn how to interrupt if you want to have any hope of getting your say in a competitive conversation. Strategies such as humor can help you. For instance, you might try raising your hand and waving it wildly both to make people laugh and to pause the conversation. You might also learn how to time your interruptions so that they do not seem rude. Cathy G. Lanier, President of Technology Solutions, Inc., states, "I'm an excellent interrupter. . . . I tend to go with the ebb and flow of meetings and am pretty good at timing my interruptions so they don't seem overly rude or pushy" (Sherman, 2005).

◆ Self-Promoting versus Self-Deprecating Speech

Consider the following comments that students made in final interviews about their team experiences. What do you think about each speaker?

> **A.** *I found that [my team] kept looking toward me. Whenever we would get bogged down, when something wasn't right, it seemed to invariably come to me to be fixed.*

B. *Well, I handled all the, uh, you know, I handled all the Web site. Basically, I built the entire Web site myself. . . . I'm the type of person, whether I fully know how to understand and know how to do it or not, I'll figure it out. I'll go ahead and take it, take the ball and go with it.*

C. *To be honest with you, I realized that the scope of this project wasn't large enough for me, so I kind of slacked off on some little things.*

D. *I can usually go into a class and kind of tell who's, you know, who's gonna do well, who's not gonna do well. Umm, who's a little quicker. Those students, I've had some of them before in other classes, and they're kind of like the lower end of the curve.*

E. *Probably Stephen made the most valuable contribution 'cause he came up with the main idea, and I know that I would never have been able to come up with that.*

F. *I did learn quite a bit about computers, and I'm saying that only because I knew so little about that beforehand. But you know, I am learning. I'm having problems publishing, but I feel I have a grasp on them.*

G. *I kind of know how to do the Web site, but I still have to have people to help me. The directions Charlotte gave me are good, but when there wasn't a direction on how to fix it, when you have something wrong, I would go outside the group.*

H. *I mean, John and Neal are really, really good at writing reports. I would be at the bottom of that list because I'm, I'm not as good at, you know, putting things together. Umm, I feel, I feel confident in creating a report. I just think that they're better at it.*

Comments A through D are examples of **self-promotional** speech, while comments E through H are examples of **self-deprecating** speech. Self-promotional speech is characterized by occasionally aggressive displays of confidence and criticism of others in order to make oneself look better. Self-deprecating speech is characterized by exaggerated displays of modesty and talking about one's own shortcomings. Both types of speech can cause major problems in groups.

Note how self-promotional talk led the speaker in comment C to see certain aspects of the project as beneath him and the speaker in comment D to view certain people as less worthy of respect. Self-promotional talk can also lead speakers to hoard certain parts of the project as their own and to exclude others from any input: this was the case with the speaker in comment B. Thus, self-promotional talk often leads to hierarchical teams in which some work is perceived as more valuable than other work and people at the top of the hierarchy can see themselves as immune to the criticisms and comments of others. This type of mind-set is so counterproductive that NASA engineers who were surveyed about problems with teams rated the statement "Some members believe that their technical status insulates their opinions from evaluation by other team members" as the number one behavior contributing to team problems (Nowaczyk, 1998).

In settings where self-promotional talk is the norm, people can be reluctant to admit weakness or ask one another for help. In student teams, this can lead to projects in which one student takes on too much but never lets the rest of the team know that the project is in danger until the end, when it is too late. In other settings, the consequences can be even higher. For instance, at one major oil company's offshore oil rigs, self-promotional norms that prized heroic accomplishments and disdained any show of weakness encouraged workers to hide mistakes; consequently, many systemic safety issues never came to light because workers did not feel comfortable discussing them. When this company purposefully tried to change the communication norms to develop an atmosphere in which workers felt comfortable productively discussing mistakes and learned to respond to criticism nondefensively, accidents were reduced by 84 percent, while productivity, efficiency, and reliability all increased (Ely & Meyerson, 2007).

Self-deprecating talk may not have such dire consequences, but it can hurt teammates' status on teams and can interfere with team productivity because it takes attention off the problem and puts it on the person and his or her abilities. This is perhaps most evident in comments E and H, in which the speakers talk excessively about how much more inferior their skills are than their teammates'. A teammate listening to this might question whether this person can be trusted with important work—and might even wonder if the speaker is indirectly asking to be given a free ride on the project. Creating this kind of doubt in your teammates' minds does nothing to help the project or yourself.

Even the other two self-deprecating comments (F and G) might make team members wonder whether the speaker is asking for reassurance—in other words, fishing for compliments. Many team members find such comments frustrating because they would rather spend their energy getting to work rather than trying to reassure and bolster the confidence of others.

Both self-promoting talk and self-deprecating talk interfere with team progress, and you should work to avoid both. Be honest about your shortcomings without focusing on them. For instance, if you are assigned a task that you are unfamiliar with, you can state, "I haven't done this before, but I'm looking forward to the challenge" or "I should be able to do that, but I want someone to look over my work just in case." Such statements suggest that you have confidence in yourself without overselling your abilities.

◆ Action-Oriented versus Holistic Problem-Solving Styles

The following comments are by students who exhibit preferences for two different problem-solving styles:

> **Bill:** *That whole first day was not productive at all. That was us spinning on our toes until the very end. The whole session was just kind of randomly hashing out what we were going to do and not actually getting anything done. That's the worst thing for me, when we just talk and talk and talk and nothing happens, you know. It's like just do it! I have nothing against going off and talking about stuff. But we didn't have time for that. We needed to start working because it was supposed to be a large-scale project and it was something that was supposed to take the whole semester and it was something that we needed to start on.*
>
> **Krista:** *I just don't like to just rush stuff. I don't like to just throw anything together, and that's what they were wanting to do. Like I said, the rest of the group was so determined to just get it done. I felt like I was the one who kept going "No, we need to go back because if we don't include everything in there he wants, he's gonna send it back. So regardless if you sit here trying to rush it, we're going to have to do it over anyway." I felt like all this was new to me, and I knew we had a time limit, but I wanted to learn too and not just do something.*

Bill's comments show that he favors an **action-oriented** problem-solving approach, in which team members jump into the details of the problem and immediately start working on a solution. By contrast, Krista appears to favor a **holistic** problem-solving approach, in which team members begin by considering the entire problem as a whole and refrain from proposing solutions until the problem is completely understood. Action-oriented problem solvers tend to concentrate on solving one piece of the puzzle at a time, whereas holistic problem solvers make sure that the end goal is always in sight.

Those who favor an action-oriented problem-solving style frequently grow impatient with holistic problem solvers and see their slowness in getting started as reflecting insecurity with the details. Being an action-oriented problem solver, Bill expresses his frustration that the group is not getting anything done. Even though the team is at the start of a semester-long project, he wants to see the group take some action.

Those favoring holistic problem solving worry that the action-oriented approach will miss the big picture—for instance, by creating a product that works but that nobody wants to buy. Krista expresses this concern when she claims that her teammates are going to put together a project that the instructor will return and ask them to do over. She wants to ensure that the group understands the requirements and end goals before they begin putting the project together.

Action-oriented problem solvers tend to learn by tinkering and trying out different solutions. This approach works well on small problems but is often less suitable for large, complex problems that require the coordination of several people because the action-oriented approach can lose sight of the big picture. Holistic problem solvers often take longer to arrive at a solution because they spend more time planning up front before they tackle the details of a problem; however, they are more likely to get the correct solution once they get started.

How Can Our Team Balance Different Problem-Solving Styles?

Both the action-oriented and the holistic problem-solving styles are important and necessary on a smoothly functioning team. However, some types of problems are more appropriately addressed by one style than the other. Your team's goal should be to try to balance these styles. The following suggestions will help you use these styles strategically:

- **The best time for holistic problem solving is at the beginning of the project.** When the group is in the early stages of the project, particularly a large project, spend some time making sure that everyone shares the same goals and that the team explores all of its options. Action-oriented problem solvers simply need to be patient at this stage. If you are concerned about deadlines, you might sketch out a brief project schedule and calculate how much time the team can afford to spend on holistic problem solving. Most holistic problem solvers will be able to switch gears and jump into the details when they feel that the time has come.

- **Be patient and strategic.** A particular problem-solving orientation may be better suited to certain tasks than to others. For instance, the group may benefit if the project manager has a more holistic problem-solving style and those working on smaller parts of the project have a more action-oriented style. Remember that differences in problem-solving styles are just that—differences—and do not reflect a person's underlying ability.

- **Refer to the team charter or task schedule to resolve conflicts.** The first two items on your team charter (see Chapter 3, "Getting Started with the Team Charter") should refer to team goals. To remind action-oriented problem solvers of the ultimate goals of the project, holistic problem solvers can refer to the goals that the team agreed on at the outset of the project. Likewise, action-oriented problem solvers can refer to the task schedule to make sure that the project stays on schedule and doesn't get derailed by too many "big picture" conversations (especially when those conversations occur near the end of the project).

◆ Gender and Communication Norms

As you read about the norms in Table 7.1, you may have thought that some of them were more characteristic of men and others more characteristic of women. Such observations may make you uncomfortable since they can lead to stereotyping. However, gender differences are worth discussing because gender influences not only how we act but also how we are perceived—and thinking about gender and communication can help us appreciate how difficult it can be to adapt to certain communication norms.

An easy way to see how gender socialization impacts communication norms is to look at body language. Take a moment to look around a classroom, lab, study area, or other public place. Can you identify differences in how men and women sit? Men typically take up more space when they sit by leaning back in their seats, sitting with legs stretched apart and extending their arms. By contrast, women tend to take up less room when they sit by sitting with knees touching and keeping their arms close to their bodies. Figure 7.4, taken from Team Video 3, illustrates some of these gender-typical differences in body language.

The men in this photograph occupy more physical space and are more likely to lean away from the group than does the one woman. Jamaal, in the foreground, leans back in his chair while extending his arm out to the group; Jim has his arm out to the side and leans slightly forward; Don

FIGURE 7.4. The effect of gender socialization on communication norms
Gender socialization appears to influence the ways in which we communicate with our body language.

places one foot across his knee (a position that men use far more frequently than do women, who are more likely to cross their legs at the knee). In contrast to the men, Tonya keeps her body close to her chair; her legs are close to each other, almost touching at the knees; and her arms are close to the center of her body. Even her hands are touching each other.

Of course, there is nothing right or wrong, or good or bad, about these different ways of sitting—but they do illustrate different norms, even different rules, governing men's and women's interpersonal behaviors. For example, if a woman sat like one of the men in the picture, she might be labeled as "unfeminine" for mimicking the body language of a male peer. Have you ever observed a woman behave in a way that you found unfeminine or a man behave in a way that you found unmanly? What specific behavior or action made you draw this conclusion? How would this behavior have appeared if someone of the opposite gender had done the exact same thing?

Not only do men and women have different norms that govern what they consider acceptable interpersonal behavior, but there are also **social rules** that affect how others perceive them if they violate these norms. As a consequence, a woman who engages in behaviors typically associated with men may be perceived in much more unflattering ways than a man would be if he did the same thing. In fact, one recent study of negotiation behaviors tested this hypothesis by asking managers to look at videotapes of men and women, all of whom were following the same script, negotiate for a higher salary. The managers perceived the female negotiator as less likable and more difficult to work with than the male negotiator, despite the fact that both had uttered the same words and followed the same nonverbal communication cues (Bowles et al., 2007).

In other words, because of these social rules, women may not be able to figure out the best way to behave by observing men's behavior, and vice versa. Thus, women who find themselves in a competitive discussion (which tends to be a more masculine communication norm) may need to find nonaggressive ways to negotiate this conversational environment without necessarily imitating men's competitive strategies. Likewise, men may need to adapt to considerate conversational styles in ways that do not necessarily mimic "feminine" strategies.

Because the same behavior can be perceived differently depending on *who* is saying it, we can't always expect other people to adjust their communication styles to what we personally perceive as normal. Although all communication styles have pros and cons, some are more *exclusionary* than others in that not everybody is equally free to engage in these behaviors. Some communication styles will produce more negative social consequences for some groups than for others.

A number of researchers have studied the impact of gender and ethnicity on communication norms:

- Men are more likely than women to have competitive speaking norms and to self-promote (Ely & Meyerson, 2007; Fletcher, 1999;

McIlwee & Robinson, 1992; Rudman, 1998; Tannen, 1990; West & Zimmerman, 1983; Wolfe & Powell, 2006).

- Women who self-promote are perceived more negatively than are men who self-promote (Bowles et al., 2007; Rudman, 1998).

- Women are more likely than men to use self-deprecating speech, a norm that is thought to hurt women in competitive workplaces (Ingram & Parker, 2002; Kitayama et al., 1997; Rudman, 1998; Tannen, 1990; Wolfe & Powell, 2006).

- African American women are less likely to be silenced by interruptions and other behaviors characteristic of competitive discussions than white women are (hooks, 1989; Kochman, 1981).

- Women are more likely to prefer online discussions (discussions that take place entirely via computer) than men are, although this preference seems to vary by ethnicity (Lind, 1999; Wolfe, 2000). Women in male-dominated teams report more satisfaction with online discussions than with face-to-face discussions (Lind, 1999), possibly because it is not possible to interrupt or talk over someone online.

- People from Asian cultures tend to favor considerate speaking norms; men who have been successful in American and European settings often have difficulty adjusting to professional environments in countries such as Japan (De Mente, 2002; Howden, 1994).

- People from the Northeast self-report more competitive communication behaviors than do people from the Midwest (Sigler, 2005).

- Men are slightly more likely than women to prefer action-oriented problem-solving styles, and women are slightly more likely to prefer holistic styles (Woodfield, 2000).

Exercises

1. Which of the communication or problem-solving styles discussed in this chapter do you tend to favor? Do you prefer the competitive speaking style or the considerate style? Are you a holistic or an action-oriented problem solver? Can you think of a time when your preferences for one style over another interfered with your ability to work productively on a team?

2. Have you ever engaged in either self-promotional or self-deprecating speech on a team? If you think back on it, how might you have spoken differently? How might this have changed the team's interactions?

3. Have you ever been on a team with someone who favored an extreme version of any of the styles discussed in this chapter? How did this person's style interfere with the team's progress? What might the team have done to minimize any negative effects that this style caused?

4. Working with a partner, go through all five *Team Writing* videos and answer the following questions for each video:

   a. Provide examples of both competitive and considerate behaviors in the video. Overall, would you describe this as a competitive or a considerate team? How might this communication style interfere with the team's success?

   b. Do you see any examples of someone being interrupted, silenced, or dismissed? What could team members have done to prevent these behaviors from occurring?

   c. Do you see any examples of self-promotional or self-deprecating behaviors? How do these behaviors seem to interfere with the team's progress?

5. Working with a partner, sit in and observe the meeting of another team in the class. Take notes on any behaviors—positive or negative—that you observe. At the end of the meeting, share notes with your partner and together type up a list of observations. Without naming names, describe the specific behaviors you observed, with quotes if possible. Share your observations with the other team.

Works Cited

Bowles, H. R., Babcock, L., & Lai, L. (2007). Social incentives for gender differences in the propensity to initiate negotiations: Sometimes it does hurt to ask. *Organizational Behavior and Human Decision Processes*, *103*, 84–103.

Commonwealthclub. (2003). *Women in business: Lessons learned*. Retrieved August 13, 2008, from http://www.commonwealthclub.org/archive/ 03/03-08women-speech.html.

Cordero, R., DiTomaso, N., & Ferris, G. F. (1996). Gender and race/ethnic composition of technical work groups: Relationship to creative productivity and morale. *Journal of Engineering and Technology Management*, *13*, 205–221.

De Mente, B. L. (2002). Sincerity, Japanese style. Excerpted from *Japanese etiquette & ethics in business*. Retrieved August 13, 2008, from http://www .apmforum.com/columns/boye49.htm.

Ely, R. J., & Meyerson, D. (2007). *Unmasking manly men: The organizational reconstruction of men's identity* (No. 07-054). Boston: Harvard Business School.

Fletcher, J. K. (1999). *Disappearing acts: Gender, power, and relational practice at work*. Cambridge, MA: MIT Press.

hooks, b. (1989). *Talking back: Thinking feminist, thinking black*. Boston: South End Press.

Howden, J. (1994). Competitive and collaborative communicative style: American men and women, American men and Japanese men. *Intercultural Communication Studies*, *4*(1), 49–58.

Ingram, S., & Parker, A. (2002). Gender and modes of collaboration in an engineering classroom: A profile of two women on student teams. *Journal of Business and Technical Communication*, *16*(1), 33–68.

Kim, H.-J. (2003). *A study of compliments across cultures*. Paper presented at the eighth annual meeting of the Pan-Pacific Association of Applied Linguistics. Retrieved August 1, 2008, from http://www.paaljapan.org/resources/ proceedings/PAAL8/pdf/pdf015.pdf.

Kitayama, S., Markus, H. R., Matsumoto, H., & Norasakkunki, V. (1997). Individual and collective processes in the construction of the self: Self-enhancement in the United States and self-criticism in Japan. *Journal of Personality and Social Psychology, 72*(6), 1245–1267.

Kochman, T. (1981). *Black and white styles in conflict*. Chicago: University of Chicago Press.

Lind, M. R. (1999). The gender impact of temporary virtual work groups. *IEEE Transactions on Professional Communication, 42*(4), 276–285.

McIlwee, J. S., & Robinson, J. G. (1992). *Women in engineering: Gender, power, and workplace culture*. Albany: SUNY Press.

Nowaczyk, R. H. (1998). *Perceptions of engineers regarding successful engineering team design* (No. NASA/CF-1998-206917 ICASE Report No. 98-9). Hampton, VA: Institute for Computer Applications in Science and Engineering.

Rudman, L. (1998). Self-promotion as a risk factor for women: The costs and benefits of counterstereotypical impression management. *Journal of Personality and Social Psychology, 74*(3), 629–645.

Sherman, A. (2005). Speak up: Is interrupting a good business tactic or just plain rude? *Entrepreneur*. Retrieved October 7, 2008, from http://findarticles.com/p/articles/mi_m0DTI/is_/ai_n15777261.

Sigler, K. A. (2005). *A regional analysis of assertiveness*. Paper presented at the annual meeting of the International Communication Association. Retrieved June 27, 2008, from http://www.allacademic.com/meta/p14806_index.html.

Tannen, D. (1990). *You just don't understand: Women and men in conversation*. New York: HarperCollins.

West, C., & Zimmerman, D. H. (1983). Small insults: A study of interruptions in cross-sex conversations between unacquainted persons. In B. Throne, C. Kramarae, & N. Henley (Eds.), *Language, gender, and society* (pp. 103–118). Rowley, MA: Newbury House.

Wolfe, J. (2000). Gender, ethnicity, and classroom discourse: Communication patterns of Hispanic and white students in networked classrooms. *Written Communication, 17*(4), 491–519.

Wolfe, J., & Powell, E. (2006). Gender and expressions of dissatisfaction: A study of complaining in mixed-gendered student work groups. *Women and Language, 29*(2), 13–21.

Woodfield, R. (2000). *Women, work, and computing*. Cambridge: Cambridge University Press.

CHAPTER 8

Troubleshooting Team Problems

In my research on teamwork, more than half of the student teams I observed ran into at least one major breakdown in the course of their project. Although following the advice in this book will help your team avoid many of these breakdowns, problems undoubtedly will still occur. This chapter summarizes some of the problems that your team might encounter and provides advice and strategies for handling these problems at the outset.

Unfortunately, many problems that arise in student teams are never addressed—or are mentioned only at the end of the project, when it may be too late. To help you address problems early, this chapter provides many examples of how you can phrase uncomfortable requests to teammates and some example e-mails you might use.

◆ Problems with Showing Up and Turning in Work

As the final deadline for his project approaches, Chad writes about the problems his group is experiencing:

> Jessica and Dave have not both shown up to class on the same day, much less on time, within the last two weeks. I am beginning to feel like a babysitter. I also feel like the weight of work has shifted onto me. Our presentation is only five days away. Dave is trying to work on a new survey, but this time for professors. Jessica doesn't have a freakin' clue what is going on. This has not been a fun week.

Resa expresses a slightly different problem at the end of her project:

> My biggest complaint is with Gene. All of the reprocessed information that he brought to class was not usable. I think I spent more time making his contributions fit than he spent doing it the first time. I tried to get his

input, but it took so long to get responses out of him and then they were worthless. . . . I really do feel that the project they are taking credit for is about 90 percent mine.

Teams should never allow problems to go on as long as Chad and Resa did. Creating a clear task schedule and having an effective project manager are the best ways to prevent the problems they experienced; nonetheless, even with these in place, you may still have problems with "slacker" (or just incompetent) teammates. This chapter presents some strategies you can use to handle specific problems with teammates who slack off.

PROBLEM

A teammate misses a meeting.

Everybody has emergencies or illnesses (or forgetfulness) that may result in missing a meeting. If any team members miss a meeting, they should contact the project manager as soon as possible to explain their absence and to ask what they missed. If they don't contact the team, the project manager can send a friendly reminder (see Figure 8.1).

If a team member routinely misses meetings, you need to take some action, such as assigning this person some extra work (see Figure 8.2). For instance, you might assign him or her a clerical task that others don't want to do. However, don't use this tactic if the team member has also missed deadlines—assigning additional work to a person who has proved to be untrustworthy may put the group even further behind. The following section outlines how to proceed if a team member misses deadlines.

TO: Jessica
FR: Chad
Subject: Today's meeting

Jessica:

We missed you at today's meeting at noon. I hope everything is okay. I've attached our minutes here. When you get a chance, could you contact me so that I can fill you in on what we did? Be sure to look at the task schedule, too, because we all have deadlines coming up.

Chad

FIGURE 8.1. Friendly reminder after a missed meeting

TO: Jessica
FR: Chad
Subject: Today's meeting and revised task schedule

Jessica:

Today was the third team meeting that you missed. To balance out the workload (since everyone is expected to attend meetings), today we decided to update the task schedule and assign you to write the transmittal letter and make photocopies for the final presentation. I've e-mailed Prof. Williams the updated task schedule and task assignment worksheet with a note that your extra workload is due to missed meetings. Please let me know if you have any concerns. I've attached the revised task schedule.

Chad

FIGURE 8.2. E-mail after a series of missed meetings
The tone is matter-of-fact, and the wording makes it clear that the project manager is implementing the group decision. However, don't use this tactic for a team member who has also missed deadlines—assigning additional work to a person who has proved to be untrustworthy may put the group even further behind.

PROBLEM

A teammate misses a deadline.

Failure to meet deadlines—a common problem for teams—is often caused by a team's failure to maintain an up-to-date task schedule. As you learned in Chapter 4, "Getting Started with the Task Schedule," the most important thing you can do to ensure that a team project runs smoothly is to maintain and publicize the task schedule. However, even with a task schedule, team members will sometimes miss deadlines—they might forget about due dates, or run into personal problems, or find that the work took longer than they anticipated. A gentle reminder is appropriate in these cases. In Figure 8.3, note how the presence of a team charter makes Jason's task easier—he simply has to remind his teammate of the consequences that everyone (including Brittany) agreed on at the beginning of the project.

The team charter should specify how long the team should wait before enforcing the consequences of a missed deadline. If at the end of this time period the team member still has not turned in his or her work (or has turned in very incomplete work), you should notify the instructor. When you do so, you don't have to point fingers; instead, just describe the situation as objectively as possible (see Figure 8.4).

Students often feel that informing the instructor of problems is "tattling" on their teammates. However, you need to think ahead to the workplace, where a team that doesn't report problems to a supervisor will face

---

TO: Brittany
FR: Jason
Subject: Sketches

Dear Brittany:

Just a reminder that your sketches were due yesterday morning. Please e-mail them as soon as possible. Remember that we agreed in our team charter that the project manager would e-mail the instructor if anything was more than 48 hours late (which would be Wednesday a.m.). If you are having some sort of personal emergency that will prevent you from doing this work, please let me know and I'll consult with the others.

Thanks,
Jason

FIGURE 8.3. A gentle reminder that a deadline has passed
Without making any accusations, this e-mail matter-of-factly reminds the team member of the consequences for late work.

severe reprimands. Your note to the instructor doesn't need to be accusatory—simply state the facts. Your instructor may respond by sending a strong reminder, removing the offending person from the team and giving the team a new charge or new deadlines, or reducing the offending person's contribution grade.

Some situations may warrant special consideration. For example, a teammate may have a serious medical or personal emergency that prevents him or her from doing the work. In these exceptional cases, the

---

TO: Professor Williams
FR: Jason
Subject: Problem with team deadlines

Dear Professor Williams:

My team is requesting your advice/help on dealing with a missed deadline. The attached task schedule shows that the initial sketches for our design were due on March 5. I have sent two reminders to Brittany (the person responsible), who said she had a cold but would get them to us by this morning. However, we still have not received the sketches, which are now almost three days late. As you know, the first draft of the project is due on Friday, and we don't quite know how to proceed. Any suggestions you have would be greatly appreciated.

Thanks,
Jason, Project Manager

FIGURE 8.4. E-mail to an instructor for a missed deadline

project manager may want to consult with the rest of the team, suggesting a way to revise the task schedule so that another team member takes over this person's deadline—with the understanding that the incapacitated team member will do additional work at the end of the project. Before you do this, however, make sure that the excuse is valid: you don't want to assign an untrustworthy team member too much work at the end of the project, when it can be difficult for the team to recover.

PROBLEM

A teammate turns in incomplete work.

Sometimes, a teammate will meet a deadline but will turn in work that is substantially incomplete. To prevent this problem, the project manager should immediately skim all work that is turned in to ensure that all the required parts are included. If anything is missing, the project manager should immediately e-mail the team member, specifying which parts are missing and giving him or her a deadline for turning in a complete draft. If a complete version is not turned in by the deadline, the project manager should notify the instructor. The next section contains sample e-mails for dealing with this situation.

PROBLEM

A teammate turns in poor-quality work.

This problem is a little more difficult to handle than the previous two because the difference between an acceptable and an unacceptable draft is often a gray area that requires a judgment call.

When a team member turns in work that the project manager feels is substantially below the group's quality standards, the project manager should contact the other team members privately and ask if anyone else agrees with this assessment. If at least one other person agrees that the team can't use the work, the project manager should e-mail the teammate who turned in the work and ask for a revision. Figure 8.5 illustrates a request for a revised draft. The request for revision should

- briefly explain why the work was considered substandard or unusable

- provide specific suggestions about resources that the teammate can consult for help

- include a specific deadline for turning in the revised work

- ask the teammate to let the project manager know immediately if he or she will not be able to make the deadline or meet the requests

TO: Gene
FR: Resa
Subject: Draft of quantitative sections

Dear Gene:

Thanks for turning in your draft on time. I've looked it over and discussed it with some of the other team members, and we think that this is not what Professor Williams is looking for. Specifically:

• The graphs don't meet the guidelines Professor Williams discussed in the "Preparing Effective Charts and Tables" lecture two weeks ago. He put his PowerPoint slides on the course Web site if you need to review them. In particular, be sure to include clear captions since he really emphasized this.

• We were confused on the differences between graphs 2, 3, and 4. Captions would really help, but a different organization might also be useful. I think it makes much more sense to include the overview graph before breaking down the results by product type. This helps the audience see the big picture first before getting into the details and would clarify how the graphs differ.

• The information on comparing costs is missing. Ashley sent this information in an e-mail last week.

• We noticed a lot of grammatical errors and typos. I know this is a draft, but it would really help if you could fix some of this before turning it in.

Thanks for taking these suggestions into consideration. Do you think you can get us a revised draft by Thursday night? Let me know ASAP if you can't make that deadline. I'll update the task schedule with this new information.

Resa, Project Manager

FIGURE 8.5. Request for revision
Note the detailed suggestions and the specific deadline. Such a request for revision should be made when a team member turns in work that the team finds unacceptable.

PROBLEM

A teammate disappears completely.

The sooner you take action when a teammate seems to have disappeared, the less likely it is that this situation will turn into a serious problem. If you believe that someone in your group has dropped out of the picture entirely, you should notify your instructor (see Figure 8.6).

TO: Professor Williams
FR: Audrey
Subject: Missing teammate

Dear Professor Williams:

Mike has missed the last three team meetings and has not responded to any of our e-mails. He hasn't missed any deadlines yet, but we are worried that he will, or that he won't understand what to do because he's missed so many meetings. We are wondering how you would like us to proceed.

If we don't hear from you by Friday (our next meeting), we'll go ahead and update the task schedule assuming that Mike is no longer part of the team. That way we won't get behind on the project. Also, we were wondering if you had any instructions or new guidelines for us now that it looks like we are becoming a three-person team.

Thanks for your help.
Audrey, Project Manager

FIGURE 8.6. E-mail notifying an instructor that a teammate is missing

◆ Problems with Personal Interactions

Midway through his project, Brian expresses some concerns about his teammates:

> Things are not going well on our team. I have heard Daniel talk about how he could be writing things so much better than Bethany and about how she is just "getting the job done." Daniel doesn't seem to trust anybody except himself. Bethany is not completely innocent either. If you listen, you'll notice that she basically shoots down most of his ideas or makes fun of them.

Jessica has more pointed things to say about one of her teammates:

> I just didn't, I didn't think that my judgment was respected by Josh at all. He never listened to anything I had to say. I didn't think that he saw me as a person in the group. He saw me as a, a female or something. . . . And I just cannot cope with somebody like that.

Teams often have problems with interpersonal conflict because teammates just don't seem to get along. This section provides advice for handling situations in which low trust or high resentment is interfering with group progress.

PROBLEM

My team doesn't trust me to do good work.

Teammates may have a number of reasons for not trusting one another to do good work. Sometimes, team members may behave in ways that make others question their competence. At other times, team members may have prejudices against certain groups or particular people. Before you assume that your team is prejudiced against you, make sure that you are not engaging in some behavior that makes them question whether you are capable of doing good work.

The following list describes behaviors that can make your team lose trust in you and provides some ways to regain respect within your team:

Are you failing to submit quality work on time? If you miss a deadline or turn in poor-quality work, your teammates may distrust your ability to do good work: you have already let them down once, and they have reason to worry that you may do it again. If your team has lost trust in you, you need to work extra hard to regain that trust. Some ways to regain trust are:

- **Turn work in early.**

- **Ask questions.** You may think that asking questions would make teammates worry about your competence, but it can often have the opposite effect. When you ask questions, your teammates know that you are working on the problem; if you are asking relevant questions, they know that you are on the right track and will likely meet deadlines. *You should never turn in work late because you are unsure about what to do.* This will ensure that your work not only is late but also may be of poor quality: the worst of both worlds. Instead, ask questions early so that you can get the help you need. If you are uncomfortable asking your team for help, make an appointment with your instructor for individual help on the task (this is what instructors are for) or seek an on-campus tutoring resource. Many schools have writing centers, where you can meet with a tutor to go over writing problems, and computer resource centers, where you can go for assistance on technical matters. In fact, many writing centers can also provide advice on preparing Web sites, PowerPoint presentations, or multimodal projects—ask when you call for an appointment.

Are you being self-deprecating or talking too much about your shortcomings? If you are always talking about how little you know, your lack of skills, how you struggle with grades, your incompetence with computers, or how smart others are in comparison to you, your teammates may believe this talk and be hesitant to trust you with major work. This is particularly the case in masculine environments in which self-promotion may be part of the culture. (See Chapter 7, "Communication Styles and Team Diversity," for more on the problems of both self-promoting and self-deprecating speech.) You don't have to talk about how great you are, but nor should you advertise your shortcomings. If you realize that your teammates have come to distrust you because you have been self-deprecating, you can:

- **Explain that you often sell yourself short and ask for more work.** Let your teammates know that even though you sometimes belittle your abilities, you still want to be challenged. Ask to be assigned additional or more challenging tasks, and offer to complete the work early so that the team doesn't have to worry about being stuck with low-quality work.

Do you appear confused or disengaged in team meetings? Take a look at Team Video 2: Shelly, Will, and Ben. When Ben viewed this video in his final team meeting, he was shocked to see how disengaged he was from the group. He said that he gave the appearance that he didn't care about the project. Judging from this behavior, Ben's teammates would have been justified in wondering whether they could trust him. If you are worried that you may be giving the wrong impression during team meetings, you can:

- **Review the task schedule and read your e-mail before the meeting.** Make sure that you know what the team is doing before you go to the meeting.

- **Start the meeting by saying something.** Show the team that you have something to say by speaking early. Ask a question or make a comment about the task schedule or about a recent e-mail that was sent. If someone has asked for feedback on a draft, make sure that you have something to say (see Chapter 6, "Revising with Others").

- **Sit forward, look up, and make eye contact.** Use body language to show that you are engaged.

Sometimes, however, your teammates may be prejudiced against you for no reason. If you believe that your teammates are reluctant to assign you challenging work because their prejudice makes them distrust your ability to do high-quality work, you can confront this distrust proactively by saying, "You don't seem to have confidence in me. I would like to take on task X. I can do it before the deadline so that I have plenty of time to redo it if the team is unhappy," or "I would like to take on task X. I promise to check with the teaching assistant [or run it past the instructor, or go to the writing center] before turning it in to the team." Such an approach lets your teammates know that you sense their prejudice but are going to turn in high-quality work anyway.

PROBLEM

My team isn't listening to me — or is taking a direction I disagree with.

Even if your teammates trust you to do good work, you may occasionally have trouble getting your ideas on the table. When team discussions are competitive, speakers with a considerate speaking norm often have difficulty making themselves heard (see Chapter 7, "Communication Styles and Team Diversity").

If you have difficulty getting your teammates to listen to you, try the following strategies:

Learn how to enter competitive conversations. To increase the likelihood that your team will listen to you in face-to-face meetings, try the following strategies:

- **Speak up early in meetings.** Be one of the first people to speak so that your teammates will get used to thinking of you as someone who has something to contribute.

- **Show that you are prepared.** Before the meeting, read all relevant information, check your e-mail, and become familiar with the task schedule. Begin the meeting by saying that you have reviewed all the materials and have some suggestions.

- **Develop strategies for dealing with interruptions.** If you get cut off when you start to speak, hold up your hand like a stop sign or say "Just a minute, I'm not done yet." (See Chapter 7, "Communication Styles and Team Diversity," for more strategies for dealing with interruptions.)

Move the conversation to writing. If you are not an assertive speaker, you might have greater success making yourself heard in writing than in a face-to-face conversation. You can't get interrupted in an e-mail. Moreover, e-mailing your thoughts gives you a chance to state your ideas without the pressure and competition of a face-to-face meeting. You may want to begin the next meeting by reminding teammates of your e-mail and summarizing your main points. Figure 8.7 illustrates how a team member moves the conversation to writing.

Prepare an alternate draft. Because it can be time-consuming, this strategy is probably a last resort. However, if you strongly disagree with what your team is doing, you can prepare another draft (or partial draft) of the document and ask an objective outsider (such as your instructor) to comment on both versions. Don't tell this person which draft is yours. Also, keep your request neutral: simply ask this person to comment on which draft he or she feels is better. Figure 8.8 illustrates this strategy.

TO: Keith, Mark
FR: Natalie
Subject: Another option for organizing

Hey all:

I've been thinking over the discussion we had in class this morning. If I understand correctly, Mark wanted to make clear that students have to do many things before they apply, but Keith was concerned that a heading for "pre-applying" would be too big and that just about everything we wanted to talk about would end up under this heading. I was thinking that a good compromise might be to try the following organization/ headings:

1. Ongoing: What should I do before my senior year?
Under this heading, we could list things like volunteering or developing a relationship with a professor.
2. The application process: What do I need to do to put my application together?
Here would go the nitty-gritty details like asking for recommendations and getting transcripts. This would be the longest section.
3. After the application is in: What can I do to prepare for the interview?
Here we can talk about the interview process.

I think this organization addresses both Keith's and Mark's concerns. Also, I want to make a case for including questions in the headings. This structure makes the document reader-friendly and shows students exactly what to expect in each section. A lot of FAQs are organized this way (and really what we're doing is preparing an FAQ of questions about the application process), so people are already familiar with the question-heading format.

Sorry I didn't bring this up in class today. Sometimes, I have trouble thinking on my feet—but I do have strong ideas about things, even if I have trouble getting them out!

If you guys like this organization, maybe Mark could send me what he wrote in class today, and I could move some things around and fill in some blanks. That way we'll have more to work with when we meet again and can use our time more efficiently. Also, we might want to assign sections to people and then meet to discuss them rather than try to do everything together in class. I think I might be able to contribute more that way, and we'd use our group time more efficiently.

Thanks,
Natalie

FIGURE 8.7. E-mail that moves the conversation to writing
Natalie uses this e-mail to suggest a specific change to the group document as well as changes in how the group works. In addition, she clarifies that she is engaged in the group, even if she is quiet during meetings. Natalie keeps her tone positive by focusing on what will be best for the group. She provides a rationale for all of her suggestions and avoids any wording that might seem accusatory.

TO: Joe, Megan
FR: Jayme
Subject: Our Web site

Joe, Megan:

We were having some disagreement over the layout of our Web site yesterday. Rather than continue to hash it out in person, I went ahead and took the liberty of preparing a version that I thought might be an improvement on the good work Joe has already done. I was thinking that when we meet tomorrow, we might ask Prof. Williams or some of the students in another group to say which of the versions they like better—or what fea-tures they like from each of these. I promise to drop my ideas if they don't like my design. I'd just like to get another opinion before we go any further. And Joe, I really appreciate what you've done for the group, even if I sometimes have suggestions for improvement!

Thanks,
Jayme

FIGURE 8.8. E-mail suggesting that the team consider an alternate draft
Jayme is careful to acknowledge that sometimes people just disagree, and she promises to drop her objections if the outside opinion doesn't support her. This strategy can be an excellent, neutral way to resolve disagreements.

PROBLEM

Other team members are not committed to a high-quality product.

Sometimes, your teammates may not be committed to producing high-quality work. However, if your group has prepared a team charter, you may be able to persuade your teammates to make changes by appealing to the goals and criteria the team agreed on at the start of the project. Base your request for changes closely on the language used in the team charter.

If the team still seems unmotivated to do high-quality work, you might ask your instructor or another knowledgeable outsider to comment on the work done so far. These comments may motivate team members to increase their efforts on the project. Or you might ask your instructor to share his or her grading rubric (a list of the criteria with which the project will be evaluated). Using this rubric, go over the project and point out specific areas where you think the team is failing to meet expectations.

PROBLEM

My teammates do and say things I find disturbing or demeaning.

Some situations are simply intolerable. If, for instance, a team member makes sexist or racist comments, you should report these to your instructor or (if you feel uncomfortable talking to the instructor) to an adviser or a faculty member of a group such as the Society for Women Engineers. These authority figures can advise you on how to handle the situation. Comments do not need to be directed to anyone in the group (or anyone in particular) to be offensive. Even generalized comments about sex or race can make teamwork uncomfortable—even when they're not meant to be taken personally.

If a teammate makes romantic advances or personal comments, you can tell the project manager privately that you feel uncomfortable with this person; you can also request that the task schedule be changed to limit your contact. It is inappropriate for someone to ask a teammate out on a date while the project is ongoing—such personal issues should wait until the project is finished. If the person making you uncomfortable is the project manager, talk to the instructor or ask another team member to intervene on your behalf. Keep in mind that in the workplace, such behavior can lead to harassment suits or worse; therefore, students need to learn what is inappropriate while they are still in school.

Other problems may be more difficult to resolve, especially when it is hard to determine whether a teammate's comments and behavior are based on prejudice, personal dislike, or some other factor. If no outright sexist or racist behavior or harassment is going on, try to resolve the problem through other strategies. To find strategies that might improve your situation, review the sections on how to deal with lack of trust or failure to listen or some of the following sections on revision.

PROBLEM

My teammates criticize my work excessively.

Sometimes, team members may be excessively harsh on someone else on the team in order to avoid work or to keep their own work out of the spotlight. If this appears to be the case, talk to the project manager about updating the task schedule and rebalancing the workload. If you feel that your teammates are using criticism to try to get you to do what should be their work, you might suggest that they be responsible for making revisions.

However, before you take any action, be sure that you are not responding defensively to justifiable and productive criticism. Allow yourself a cooling-off period (24 hours if possible) before taking any action. Then return to the criticism to see whether it is justified. Perhaps your teammate has pointed out a legitimate problem but has suggested an incorrect solution—or has misidentified the problem. Take a critical look at your writing and see if something needs to be changed, even if it's not exactly what your teammate pointed out. If, ultimately, you feel that a teammate is treating you unfairly, ask someone else on the team whether he or she has also noted this behavior. This person may be able to help you find a solution.

◆ Problems with Revision

Erin describes in her final interview how a teammate resisted any revisions that other team members wanted to implement:

> Well, Jin did the first draft of the Web site, and she said we could revise it, but then anytime we wanted to do something different, it was "No, don't do that, you can't do that," that sort of thing. And I remember it was funny because initially she told a story about how when she was in preschool, a little boy was sitting next to her coloring a picture, and she grabbed the picture from him and said, "I'll do it for you. It will be better this way." She told that story, and it kind of fit into the project.

Ben, meanwhile, had the opposite problem with his team:

> And I was disappointed. I thought we'd get a chance to improve, but everybody was just like "yeah, yeah, that's good." So there was no motivation to revise.

Teams often run into conflict when they get into the nitty-gritty details of making revisions. This section describes strategies for handling those who either don't want to listen to their teammates' suggestions for revisions or don't feel comfortable suggesting revisions to their peers' work.

PROBLEM

Team members are not open to revisions to their work— or team members ignore the suggestions I make for revision.

Sometimes, you may suggest revisions to material that a teammate has prepared, only to have these suggestions ignored or dismissed. If a teammate ignores your suggestions or just acts as if your feedback doesn't exist, first you need to find out *why* your suggestions were ignored. A teammate might ignore your suggestions because he or she (1) agrees that the suggestions would improve the work but doesn't feel that they are worth the time or effort to implement, (2) disagrees with the suggestions, or (3) overlooked, missed, or forgot about the suggestions. If you want to find out which of these three reasons applies, send a simple "reminder" e-mail to your teammate (see Figure 8.9), with a copy to other team members if necessary.

TO: Jin
FR: Thomas
CC: Josh, Eli
Subject: Revisions to results section

Dear Jin:

I sent some suggestions for the results section last week, but in the revised draft I saw that none of my suggestions were implemented. In case you didn't receive them, I'm attaching them to this e-mail. If you think they're off-base, please let me know.

Josh, could you add a discussion of these revision suggestions to our next team meeting? In our team charter, we said that we would follow all the guidelines for presenting results that Professor Williams gave us. Although I think Jin's draft is a good start, I don't think it contains everything that Professor Williams wants.

Thanks,
Thomas

FIGURE 8.9. E-mail reminding a teammate about suggestions for revision
Thomas acknowledges the possibility that his teammate didn't receive his earlier suggestions. By asking the project manager to put his revisions on the agenda, Thomas also puts subtle pressure on the team to at least *consider* his suggestions. In addition, he appeals to the team charter to support his request that the team consider his ideas.

If your teammate agrees with the suggestions but doesn't want to implement them, ask the team to discuss whether the suggestions are worth implementing. To make sure that the ideas are discussed, ask the project manager to put this item on the agenda for a future meeting, or ask team members to comment on your suggestions via e-mail. If the changes will be time-consuming, the team may need to consider updating the task schedule and redistributing the workload.

If your team agrees with your suggested revisions but decides that they are not worth the time to implement, you may need to take on additional work to ensure that the project is done right. However, make sure that the project manager updates the task schedule to show the extra work you have done.

If the team disagrees with your suggestions and you feel they are worth pursuing, refer to the section "My team isn't listening to me—or is taking a direction I disagree with." In this situation, you might want to create an alternate draft and ask the instructor or someone else to make a judgment call (see Figure 8.8).

PROBLEM

My team is destroying my work.

Occasionally, you may hand off a document to a teammate, only to have that person make radical revisions that you disagree with. In this situation, using Track Changes or another software tool that keeps a history of revisions can be quite useful because everyone can go back and recover material that may have been lost during another person's revisions (see Chapter 6, "Revising with Others").

If you feel that your teammates' revisions *weaken* rather than improve your work, state the reasons for your position and ask the team to reconsider (see Figure 8.10).

You should always feel free to ask teammates to reconsider revisions they have made to your work, but sometimes you need to accede to the group and follow the team's decision. To be sure that you are not just being defensive about your own work, wait 24 hours before responding

---

TO: Rene
FR: Gene
CC: Brittany
Subject: Revisions to proposal

Dear Rene:

I just looked over the revisions you made to my draft—I definitely think there are some good changes in here that improve the proposal. However, I noticed that you changed all of the headings from short sentences to single words or phrases. I'd like to offer two reasons for turning them back into sentences:

1. The sentence headings help readers skim the document. That way, if they just read the headings, they'll get an idea of what our proposal is about without having to read any of the details.
2. One of the examples Professor Powell showed us in class had sentence headings. Of all the examples, I thought that one was the best organized, and she seemed to like it too.

Let me know what you think. Maybe Brittany could also comment on which style she prefers?

Thanks! I'll see you in class.
Gene

FIGURE 8.10. E-mail asking the team to reconsider some revisions
Gene is careful to praise Rene's revisions before objecting to some of them. He provides clear, reader-based reasons for asking the team to reconsider these revisions.

to the revisions. Then, before you respond, read the revisions again and see whether they do in fact improve the document.

If the team reaches an impasse and cannot agree on revisions to a document, a good strategy is to ask an outsider (such as an instructor or another member of the class) to look over the different versions and comment on which version he or she prefers. The team should agree in advance to abide by that person's decision.

PROBLEM

Team members are not giving adequate feedback.

If a teammate has been assigned to provide suggestions on (or make revisions to) your work and simply corrects a few typos or says that it "looks good," you need to encourage your teammate to give more thorough feedback. In such cases, you can try to obtain feedback by asking some specific questions, as shown in Figure 8.11.

    TO: Carlos
    FR: Marissa
    CC: Josh
Subject: Feedback

Dear Carlos:

I just looked over the suggestions you made to my draft. I'll definitely make the corrections you pointed out, but there are a few "big issues" I was worried about that I was hoping you could comment on.

1. I was wondering if you could double-check the graphs I've provided and make sure that I copied all the numbers correctly. Have I forgotten anything on the axis labels? Do you think that a different graph format might be a better representation? Prof. Williams made a really big deal about graphs in class lectures, so I want to make sure they're okay.
2. Right now I've presented speed first (since it's the biggest difference) and then accuracy, but I was wondering if accuracy should go first because it's more important than speed. What do you think?
3. Could you take another look at the assignment sheet and make sure that we haven't left anything off?

Thanks for taking another look at this. I want to make sure we get the benefits of a team project by having as many "eyes" critique this as possible.

Thanks,
Marissa

FIGURE 8.11. E-mail requesting more thorough feedback
Marissa asks her teammate to comment on several specific questions. Her e-mail focuses on what she would like to happen in the future rather than on what went wrong in the past.

Even with a reminder and another invitation to provide feedback, some teammates may neglect this duty. If so, you may want to contact the project manager and ask that another teammate (or the project manager) be assigned to read and comment on the draft. Make sure that the task schedule gets updated so that this person receives credit for the additional work he or she has done.

PROBLEM

I'm not sure how to give good feedback to team members.

Giving feedback to others can be unnerving—especially if you are worried that your writing skills may not be as good as theirs. Using Track Changes or another software tool that records a history of revisions can be very useful because your teammates can easily go back and recover the original document if they disagree with your revisions (see Chapter 6, "Revising with Others").

Even if you are unsure of your writing abilities, you can take a few steps to ensure that you give good-quality feedback:

- Read the assignment sheet and note *everything* that needs to appear in your document. Then review the document carefully and make sure that nothing has been left out.

- Try to obtain a copy of the grading rubric (a sheet that lists the evaluation criteria) that your instructor will be using to evaluate the project, and note any areas where you think the project might be lacking. Even if you are not sure how to fix these deficiencies, simply pointing them out might prod other team members to think of ways to improve the document.

- Visit your campus writing center and ask a tutor to help you find things to critique. Bring a copy of the assignment instructions (and grading rubric if you have one) so that the tutor can get a general idea of what your instructor expects. Even if the tutor doesn't know all the specifics of the assignment, he or she should be able to point out some weak aspects of your document and to note general writing issues such as poor grammar, inconsistent logic, or poor organization.

Exercises

1. Review the following comments, which teammates made about one another midway through their project. How would you handle the situation if you were Carlos and Veronica? What can Mike do to regain the trust and respect of his teammates?

    Carlos: It seems to me that Mike isn't very involved. Mike joins in the discussion we have during class time about the project, but he seems to put very little work in outside of class. After we were working on the project proposal in lab, he told me he felt his voice was not being heard, but then he did not post any changes to the project proposal at the time we all agreed to post our changes.

Mike: The first time we met to work on a document, I felt ignored by the rest of the group. I spoke my concerns to some of the others, however, and have confidence that it won't happen again. . . . I feel like I've not been doing anything. . . . For the most part, the aspect of the project that I've been assigned to work on is on hold until I get more information from the rest of the group.

Veronica: The team is working all right together—mostly everything is getting done. The only noteworthy incident would involve Mike, who seems to never know what is going on. He was in charge of compiling the proposal, and we had to extend the date many times. . . . He even said he couldn't write it because he was missing some info that Carlos had e-mailed out two weeks ago.

2. Two group members exchanged the following e-mails after spending a class period arguing unsuccessfully about changes to a short proposal. This situation does not fit neatly into the scenarios covered in this chapter; however, much of the advice in this chapter can be modified to fit this situation.

TO: Jayme, Megan
FR: Joe
Subject: Time

I have been monitoring our group meetings to see how much we accomplish. We always start out well, but then we waste everybody's time by bickering over the littlest stuff. So we always end up taking waaaay longer than is needed for the task. We spend so much time on little stuff that it is pathetic. There is no reason that a proposal that is only one and a half pages long should take 25 minutes to revise. As adult college students, we should have revised that in 15 to 20 minutes.

Here is another example: we sat in class yesterday for almost 45 minutes discussing the proposal. So what did we really accomplish? Nothing! Because, here again, we were arguing over "you say lemons, I say oranges." Last time I looked, both of those are fruits!

So let's stop wasting all of our time bickering. I propose that we set a time limit for how long a discussion should take. Then, when we reach that time limit, we should just vote. That's it. No more discussion.

Joe

FIGURE 8.12. E-mail exchange between teammates

TO: Joe
FR: Jayme
CC: Megan
Subject: Time

In response to your message, I don't think time is the issue. If it takes two hours to write the proposal, then it takes two hours to write the proposal. It took me at least that amount of time to write the first progress report, but I wanted to make sure it was done right.

If I have a problem with something that has my name on it, I want to feel free to voice my opinion. ALL of our opinions ARE worthy because we are all part of the group. I agree that I don't want to argue. The only way to accomplish this is to be open to one another's ideas and not shut them out because we don't have the time to hear them. That causes tension and in the long run is less time-efficient.

If time is the biggest concern, then perhaps we need to give the jobs to those of us in the group who are willing to take that time to get the job done right, the first time.

Jayme

FIGURE 8.12. *(continued)*

After reading the e-mails in Figure 8.12, answer the following questions:

a. What do you think about the tone of each of these e-mails? How do you think the recipients responded to them? What do you suspect was the outcome of this exchange?

b. The sample e-mails throughout this book try to phrase problems in nonaccusatory language. Reread these sample e-mails and find some wording that Joe and Jayme might have used to make their exchange less accusatory.

c. Overall, what strategies could these students have used to avoid this problem in the first place? Now that the problem has occurred, what strategies could they use to get their team back on the right track?

Appendices

Peer Evaluation Questionnaire

At the end of your project, answer the following questions about your teammates and your own contributions to the project.

1. List *everything* that each member of the team (including yourself) contributed to the project. Be as specific as possible.

2. For each member of the team (including yourself), list the single most important contribution that he or she made to the project.

3. What advice would you give to each of your teammates to help them improve their teamwork skills?

4. Would you want to work with these teammates again on a future project? Why or why not? (Your answer is confidential.)

You can also download a copy of this questionnaire from the *Team Writing* Web site at <bedfordstmartins.com/teamwriting>.

Sample Meeting Minutes

Following are three versions of the meeting minutes from one four-person team. All three versions contain the same information. Which version—version 1, 2, or 3—do you think will be the most effective for keeping the team on track? Why?

Version 1

From: **Jason**
To: **Team**
Subject: **Team meeting—Monday, 3/2/09**

Present: Susan, Jeff, Karen, Jason

Karen started us off by showing us a Web site about oil-tanker transportation. We looked at that for five minutes, and then Jason suggested we review the draft Jeff prepared. Jason noted some incomplete sentences. Susan also noticed some minor grammatical errors. Karen suggested moving the information on oil transportation closer to the beginning. Jason agreed. Susan and Jeff also thought this was a good idea but felt that jumping right into the details on transportation would be too abrupt. The others agreed that the current introduction should remain, but Karen thought that it should be minimized since our audience would already know this information. Jeff liked the current introduction because it has emotional appeal and would catch our audience's attention. Jason and Susan weren't sure which version would be best. Karen suggested that we prepare two different versions and ask the instructor which one would be best for our audience. Jason volunteered to set up a meeting with the instructor later in the week, but Jeff and Karen didn't have copies of their schedules with them. All team members will e-mail Jason tonight with a copy of their schedules. Karen volunteered to write up a revised draft and e-mail it out to the team by Wednesday night. Everybody will read this draft and show up on Thursday with comments.

Jeff suggested that the team begin working on the next section of the proposal. Susan, Karen, and Jason thought that we needed to include information on costs. Jeff thought that we should look at SPCC regulations next but agreed that costs were also a high priority. Susan's uncle works for Texaco and can provide us with some information on costs. Jason volunteered to draft a section on costs by next Tuesday. Jeff and Susan both have a calculus test on Wednesday and can't work much on the project until then. We set up our next team meeting for Thursday at 1:00 p.m.

Version 2

From: **Jason**
To: **Team**
Subject: **Team meeting—Monday, 3/2/09**

Present: Susan, Jeff, Karen, Jason

To Do:
Everyone: E-mail Jason tonight with your schedule for Friday and Monday.
Karen: Implement the changes the team made on the research review. E-mail revised draft to team by Wednesday.
Jason: Set up meeting with instructor for Friday or Monday.
Susan: Draft a section on costs by next Tuesday.
Everyone: Read the draft Karen e-mails us and show up on Thursday with comments.

Dates: Next team meeting is on Thursday, 3/5, at 1:00 p.m.

Decisions:

1. **Revisions to research review**
   We spent most of the meeting discussing Jeff's draft. We decided to
   (1) move the information on oil transportation closer to the beginning.
   (2) prepare two different versions of the introductory section—one with the current emotional introduction on the environmental impacts of oil spills and one with the abbreviated introduction that doesn't repeat information our audience already knows. We will ask the instructor to decide which works better for our audience.
   (3) make grammatical corrections, especially fixing incomplete sentences.

   Karen will make the changes the team suggested and e-mail out a revised version by Wednesday night. We should all read it and come in on Thursday with comments.

2. **Meeting with the instructor**
   Jason will arrange a meeting with the instructor to discuss the two drafts. We all need to e-mail him tonight with times we are available.

3. **Costs**
   We decided that the next step is to estimate the costs of modifying the oil tankers. Susan will research this information and draft a section on costs by next Tuesday.

4. **EPA Web site**
   Karen found some good information about oil transportation on the EPA Web site. The URL is www.epa.gov/oilspill/.

Next meeting (3/5):
   (1) Discuss Karen's revisions to research review.
   (2) Verify meeting time with instructor.
   (3) Discuss costs section if there's time.

Version 3

From: Jason
To: Team
Subject: Team meeting—Monday, 3/2/09

Present: Susan, Jeff, Karen, Jason

The meeting was called to order by Karen at 1:05 p.m.

1. Karen showed us a Web site with good information. The URL is www.epa.gov/oilspill/.

2. The group discussed Jeff's draft. Jason and Susan noted some grammatical errors. Karen thought the information on the environmental impact of oil spills should be condensed. Jeff objected, stating that the current introduction provided emotional appeal and would grab the reader's attention.

3. Karen moved that we prepare two versions of the introduction section and volunteered to complete this task by Wednesday night. The motion was agreed to by the rest of the group.

4. Jason moved that the group set up a meeting with the instructor and volunteered for this task. This motion was agreed to by the rest of the group. All team members need to e-mail Jason with their schedule tonight.

5. Jeff moved that we work on the costs section next. Susan informed the group that her uncle works for Texaco. Susan moved that she will get information on costs from him and draft a costs section by next Tuesday. This motion carried unanimously.

6. Our next team meeting is on Thursday at 1:00 p.m.

The meeting adjourned at 1:50 p.m.

Responses and Outcomes for
Team Video 1: Mark, Natalie, and Keith

The following information is based on individual interviews conducted with Mark, Natalie, and Keith at the end of their team project. In addition to commenting on the project in general, each of them viewed this video. This video was also viewed by several managers with at least 10 years of professional experience supervising teams.

What did the students think about their team?

Keith was the most positive about the project and the group. He described himself as the group's leader and the "creative impetus" behind the project, Mark as the most hardworking and responsible group member, and Natalie as a "tertiary" group member who was too busy to contribute much to the project. Keith's perceptions contradict those of his teammates, largely because Keith valued in-class contributions more than work done outside the class. In fact, Keith did not produce any material outside of class, and his contributions were limited to the types of in-class exchanges you see in the video. This tendency to inflate the importance of face-to-face discussions over work that is contributed independently is a common problem of student teams.

Mark was also fairly positive about the project. Although he was occasionally frustrated with Keith, he generally enjoyed arguing with him and felt that he and Keith shared a leadership role in the group. Mark described Natalie as a reliable group member who, although she frequently missed class, completed a substantial amount of work outside of class and ultimately contributed more than Keith did to the project. He observed that sometimes Natalie may have felt "run over" by himself and Keith. However, when he watched this video at the end of the project, he expressed surprise at *how much* he and Keith were shutting Natalie out.

Natalie, unlike her teammates, described the group project as a very negative experience. She felt that the group spent too much time focusing on small details and as a consequence ended up rushing through and shortchanging parts of the project that she felt were the most important and most interesting to her personally. Although she enjoyed working

131

with Mark, whom she described as reliable and the clear leader of the group, she found Keith impossible to work with because she felt he did not respect her. She commented:

> I try to talk to people like that, but when I sense that I'm not being listened to or it's just being passed over, I'd rather just not waste my breath so I usually just kept to myself a lot of times. . . . I just didn't, I didn't think that my judgment was respected by Keith at all. . . . I just didn't think that he saw me as a person in the group.

Because she found working with Keith so difficult, Natalie eventually stopped attending class and instead e-mailed her contributions directly to Mark. When Natalie viewed this video clip at the end of the project, she commented:

> That's what they're saying. I mean, you heard the man, that's what they were saying, and that's not what they were saying. Keith was trying to say that, I don't know, I never knew what he was trying to change. I don't, there were things that he would always try to change, and it did not need to be changed. . . . I was so mad there I stopped even listening to what he was saying.

What did managers have to say about this team interaction?

Ken West, Operations Research Manager: *What I saw there is they were all trying to do the same thing together. . . . It looked like Keith was a "this is how you do it" type, while they had Mark doing it, and they might have been better off to split out and have everybody go off and write things separately, then get back together and review the intermediate sections. . . . It looked like they were trying to write together, and in the environment that they were in, it was not really conducive to having all three of them participate in the project, and as a result I think Natalie was being left out.*

Rene Stone, Computer Systems Manager: *Keith and Mark are acting like they're racing to some finish line. They're focusing on editing and writing text and producing it. They don't have time for the big picture. . . . I would counsel them to slow down, sit at a table, and come up with a strategy—not go over it with one person at the screen, the other two behind them. It's hard to have a civilized conversation like that.*

Given how upset Natalie was with her team, what would you advise her to do?

Stone: *She's going to have to do something to get their attention. I would try to get the computer seat because they both want to be* *controlling the machine. That would get her inside of their circle for a starter. And then I would try to slow it down so when they say something, I would repeat it back to take the urgency out of it.*

Interviewer: *If that didn't work, what would you recommend?*

Stone: *Go to the instructor and say, "I don't see that I have a role in this. There might be something else I should work on." Or, "Is there something else you want me to do on this project because they don't appear to need me?"*

Responses and Outcomes for Team Video 2: Shelly, Will, and Ben

The following information is based on individual interviews conducted with Shelly, Will, and Ben at the end of their team project. In addition to commenting on the project in general, each of them viewed this video. This video was also viewed by an instructor with experience in guiding team projects.

What did the students think about their team?

Shelly was largely satisfied with the project and the way the team divided the work, which she described as going down the list of information required for the proposal and dividing the tasks at random by assigning them to "Shelly, Will, Ben, Shelly, Will, Ben." She felt that the project ran smoothly, although at times she would have liked to review information before her teammates turned it in.

Will described Shelly as "pretty much taking charge" and doing a good job as leader; he described Ben as doing "exactly what he was asked but not much more than that." Will expressed some dissatisfaction with what the team turned in, saying that "the style is still reasonable but the message kind of gets lost. There's a continuity problem." He felt that by handing out five copies of a 20-page document, Shelly deterred him from critiquing anything. As Will said:

> I reviewed the sections to make sure there weren't any gross errors. But looking at it, there's that section I was talking about and a couple of typos and a couple of weird sentence structure things, but nothing that's a crisis. And to print out another five copies of that at 20 pages apiece, I didn't want to put her through the trouble of it.

However, Will never expressed any of his dissatisfaction to his teammates because he doesn't like confrontation and felt that the final document was "acceptable." Overall, Will described the team as "just three people who happened to turn in one thing."

Ben also noted that the teammates did not critique one another's work. He wished that the project could have been more of a learning experience because he did not really understand the content of the parts of the proposal that his teammates wrote. When Ben was asked about his body language in the video and his tendency to sit apart from his teammates, he said, "That's a good question. I guess I like, kind of like being on the outside looking in." Still, he worried that he might be giving "an impression that I don't really care 'cause I am not part of the group. But really I am. I was just trying to sit back and, uh, listen to what they were saying."

What did an instructor have to say about this team interaction?

John Wang: *Well, they're not fighting, but they're not really collaborating either. They have no plan and are just kind of doing everything by the seat of their pants. Nobody knows what the others are doing. . . . I don't know, but it seems to me like it's going to be a very disjointed project. . . . At an absolute minimum, any document should go through one round of review, but they're not even doing that. I would describe this as a very weak team.*

Responses and Outcomes for Team Video 3: Jamaal, Jim, Don, and Tonya

The following information is based on observations of this student team and individual interviews conducted with Jamaal, Jim, Don, and Tonya at the end of their team project.

How did this project turn out?

The short clip you saw of team members dividing up tasks shows an apparently friendly group: there is little visible tension, everyone is volunteering for tasks, and the overall atmosphere seems easygoing and collegial. At the end of the project, most of the team members were still very enthusiastic and positive about how well their team had performed.

However, this group had one major problem: Don completely plagiarized his section of the report from the Internet. Only one group member (Jamaal) was aware of this, but Jamaal did not say anything to his teammates because he assumed that the instructor would not penalize the entire group if he discovered the plagiarism. Both Tonya and Jim knew that early on in the project Don had cut-and-pasted information from the Internet onto a handout that he had given to the group, but both of them assumed that he would consolidate this information on the final draft and put it in his own words. However, neither of them did more than skim the final draft for typos. Tonya volunteered that she did not read her teammates' final contributions carefully because she was "so confident that . . . they could write and they were very articulate. [She] didn't think [she] would be right in telling them to change things."

What lesson should you learn from this team's outcome?

This group illustrates that teamwork is much more than face-to-face communication. The group's face-to-face interactions, while far from flawless, do not hint at the major disaster of this team's final project. Although face-to-face interactions are important, they do not necessarily reflect the quality of a team's written output. A person's ability to communicate orally does not necessarily translate into good writing ability (or, in this case, writing ethics)—many people are good speakers but poor writers. Having oral conversations is not a substitute for critically reading and responding to a written draft.

Another variation on the problem of focusing on oral communication at the expense of written communication is reported by Rebecca Burnett (1996), who observed a 13-student cooperative learning (or co-op) team doing an internship at a major engineering research and development corporation. The students had held many oral conversations with one of the chemists in the lab and, based on these conversations, thought they were proceeding in the right direction—only to have this same chemist respond to their final draft by saying that their work was completely unacceptable and showed that they did not understand critical aspects of the basic technology process. When team members asked the chemist why he hadn't mentioned these problems during previous conversations, he responded that until he had something to read—a coherent text that laid out ideas, explanations, and recommendations—he had no way of knowing about the fundamental gaps in their understanding.

In Burnett's study, the students' manager similarly noted how the process of simply drafting the table of contents revealed problems in the project: "It was in the process of deciding to put something on paper that . . . these vast differences in concepts started coming out." Reflecting back, one of the students on the team agreed with the manager: "The structure of the report should have been the first thing that we did, even though we didn't have . . . a lot of knowledge about [what] was going to be in it."

These comments reflect the importance of tackling the written part of a project *early* (perhaps even with a straw document—see Chapter 2, "Project Management") and of continually receiving feedback and making revisions on this document. If the students in Team Video 3 had had a stronger revision process and a commitment to truly revise and give feedback to one another, the plagiarism could have been caught before the project was submitted.

Work Cited

Burnett, R. (1996). "Some people weren't able to contribute anything but their technical knowledge": The anatomy of a dysfunctional team. In A. H. Duin & C. J. Hansen (Eds.), *Nonacademic writing: Social theory and technology* (pp. 123–156). Mahwah, NJ: Lawrence Erlbaum Associates.

Responses and Outcomes for Team Video 4: David, Veronica, and Adam

The following information is based on individual interviews conducted with David, Veronica, and Adam at the end of their team project. In addition to commenting on the project in general, each of them viewed this video. This video was also viewed by a manager with experience in supervising team projects.

What did the students have to say about this project?

Veronica was initially frustrated with the group and had considered asking the instructor to place her in a different group. She explained why she appreciated the instructor's intervention: "Actually at first I was thinking that I was wrong. I was thinking that maybe I wasn't understanding her right or maybe I just needed to be quiet. . . . If she hadn't come over, I think I would have been just isolated." However, by the end of the project, Veronica felt that "the group began to value [her] opinion" and gave her "a fair say in the finalization of the documents."

David was initially upset by the instructor's intervention; he felt that that the instructor, by siding with Veronica, was taking on a "guys against girls" role. However, upon later reflection, he realized that he might have "come on a little too strong." So for the remainder of the project, he "held back" and tried to let others give their input: "I just didn't talk as much, that's the main thing. . . . I sat back sometimes and let other people sit up. . . . And I let other people finish their sentences and tried to give them adequate feedback for what's said."

Adam noted that the group was initially pressed for time because teammates' schedules were incompatible and that the group did not really consider having teammates create drafts independently and then revise one another's work. He agreed that Veronica was overlooked initially and said that he spoke to David privately after class about trying to include everyone.

What did a professional manager have to say about this team interaction?

Rene Stone, Computer Systems Manager: *I thought Veronica did a good job trying in that first segment. David was blowing her off, and she said, "Well, wait a minute. I want to do some part of it. This is supposed to be a team effort." So she was giving the message, but he wasn't hearing it from her. He only heard it from the instructor, and even then he kind of rejected it too.*

Interviewer: *So what would you do if you were a manager of this team?*

Stone: *I would also counsel them that it was important to me that everybody have skills and everybody contribute in private because I wanted input from all of them and that it was going to make it a better product. And I would try to convince David that it was going to be a better product that way. And another tactic would be to make a blatant suggestion that he let the other two do it and then he revise. And that way he would not be involved until it was his turn, and his turn would be clear.*

The second segment is much better. They found a way to get him to share—which is getting him off the keyboard. He's listening, and they're being encouraging and saying good things and not just negative. But the Adam guy was left out. They could have asked him more for his opinions and repeat what he said. That would encourage him to speak louder and to be more engaged. He's sitting physically apart. But they're vastly improved over the first one.

Responses and Outcomes for Team Video 5: Jayme, Megan, and Joe

Several professional managers and instructors viewed Team Video 5 and offered their comments and advice.

What are your thoughts on this group?

Ken West, Operations Research Manager: (laughing) *I've seen this so many times. Whether he is or not, Joe has set himself to be the technical expert. I don't know whether it's because "I'm the guy and you two are the girls," or whatnot, but he's making all kinds of blanket statements out there that have no basis whatsoever!* (laughing) *Joe is being obstinate and not listening, and the girls are not being successful at convincing him. They're putting forth their ideas, but he's just not seeing it.*

Tim Monroe, Deputy Chief Traffic Engineer: *The guy's not listening well. I have the idea that he has things set in his mind already and he's not even trying to understand what their point is. Just because you're technically better at getting a color up on the screen doesn't mean necessarily it's got to be your color. . . . He needs to realize that other people read this thing and it's not necessarily technical people that you're trying to communicate to.*

What would you recommend to this team?

Ken West: *At this point in time, the best thing to do is bring in a third party. Bring in somebody else and say, "Just take a look at this and give us an honest opinion of what you think about it." In my world, I just bring in the user, and the user takes a look at it and says that they like it or they don't like it. . . . They could also try to set some ground rules about how they are going to handle disagreements. They could try majority vote, but in this particular case that could also lead to some stalemates because Joe is likely to say, "Well, you two are just ganging up on me, so I'll refuse to play."*

Carla Anderson, Technical Writing Instructor: *Well, they seem to have decided that they're going to take a "majority rules" approach, but Joe is really unhappy with that. Based on what I've seen here, I don't think he's ever going to hear what the women are saying. . . . I would recommend that they prepare two or three versions of the layout and then ask the instructor to comment on which one is best. Or find some other way of bringing the instructor into the process. Joe might hear things from an authority that he won't hear from his teammates. Plus, if he continues to act like this in front of the instructor, they have found a neutral way to alert the instructor to problems in the team.*

Sample Documents

Keeping Your Team Organized

Communicating about Team Meetings

Communicating about the Revision Process

Communicating about Deadlines

Communicating with Your Instructor